**Houghton Mifflin Harcourt**

# JOURNEYS

### Program Consultants

Shervaughnna Anderson · Marty Hougen
Carol Jago · Erik Palmer · Shane Templeton
Sheila Valencia · MaryEllen Vogt

### Consulting Author · Irene Fountas

Cover illustration by Bill Cigliano.

Printed in the U.S.A.

ISBN 978-0-54-454337-9

7 8 9 10  0918  23 22 21 20 19 18 17 16
4500624094          B C D E F G

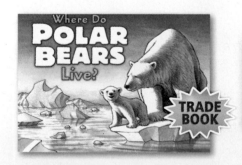

**Where Do Polar Bears Live?**
INFORMATIONAL TEXT
*by Sarah L. Thomson • illustrated by Jason Chin*

# UNIT 5 Changes, Changes Everywhere

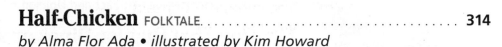

### Exploring Space Travel
INFORMATIONAL TEXT
*by Laura Hamilton Waxman*

# Be a Reading Detective!

**Welcome, Reader!**

Your help is needed to find clues in texts. As a **Reading Detective**, you will need to **ask a lot of questions** to understand what you are reading. You also need to read carefully to find **evidence**, or **clues**, to figure things out.

**☰ myNotebook**

As you read, mark up the text. Save your work to **myNotebook**.

- Highlight details.
- Add notes and questions.
- Add new words to **myWordList**.

- Ask questions that start with *who*, *what*, *where*, *why*, and *how*.

- Figure out the meanings of words you do not know.

- Look for clues in the author's words, the pictures, and the captions.

**Let's do it!**

# Heroes and Helpers

**Stream to Start**

> 66 To be afraid and to be brave is the best kind of courage of all. 99

— Alice Dalgliesh

## Performance Task Preview

At the end of this unit, you will think about two of the texts you have read. Then you will use information from the texts to write a story about an adventure you take!

fyi
hmhfyi.com

1

Channel One News®

9

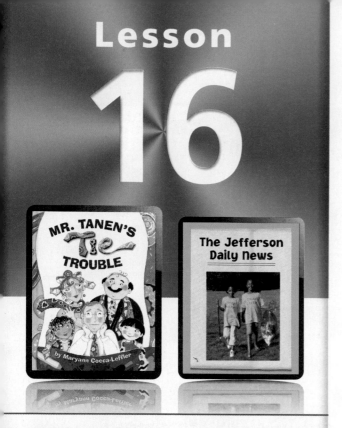

**Talk About Words**
Work with a partner. Use the Vocabulary words in new sentences that tell about the photos. Write the sentences.

**☰ myNotebook**

Add new words to **myWordList**. Use them in your speaking and writing.

# Vocabulary in Context

▶ Read each **Context Card**.

▶ Use a Vocabulary word to tell about something you did.

**1    received**
The boys received some money for raking leaves in the yard.

**2    account**
The girl opened a bank account with the money from her allowance.

### 3 budget

A budget is a plan for how you should spend your money.

> My budget for the Field Trip
> I have $11.
> I will spend $4 on lunch.
> I will spend $5 on souvenirs.
> I will spend $2 on a snack.

### 4 disappointed

He was disappointed, or sad, that he would not be able to buy the book.

### 5 chuckled

Her dad chuckled when he saw her tiny piggy bank.

### 6 staring

The girl was staring at the money. Should she save it or spend it?

### 7 repeated

The car wash was such a big success that the class repeated it in May.

### 8 fund

The players got new shirts by raising money for the team fund.

# Read and Comprehend

✓ **TARGET SKILL**

**Story Structure** The characters, setting, and plot of a story make up the **story structure**. The **setting** is where and when the story takes place. The **characters** are the people in the story. The **plot** is what happens in the story.

As you read *Mr. Tanen's Tie Trouble*, think about what the important events are. You can use a story map like the one below to show the main parts of the story.

| Characters | Setting |
|---|---|
| **Plot** | |

✓ **TARGET STRATEGY**

**Infer/Predict** Use clues, or text evidence, to figure out more about story parts.

## Helping Others

There are many ways to help other people. Holding the door for someone is one small way to help a person. Visiting someone who is sick can help make him or her feel better. Taking care of family pets or doing chores can help out at home. Helping others makes them feel good, and it can make you feel good, too!

You will read about a principal who helps his school in *Mr. Tanen's Tie Trouble*.

### 💬 Think | Pair | Share

When have you helped others? Talk about it with a partner.

▶ Who did you help and why?

▶ Has anyone ever helped you?

Share your answers with the class. Listen carefully to others.

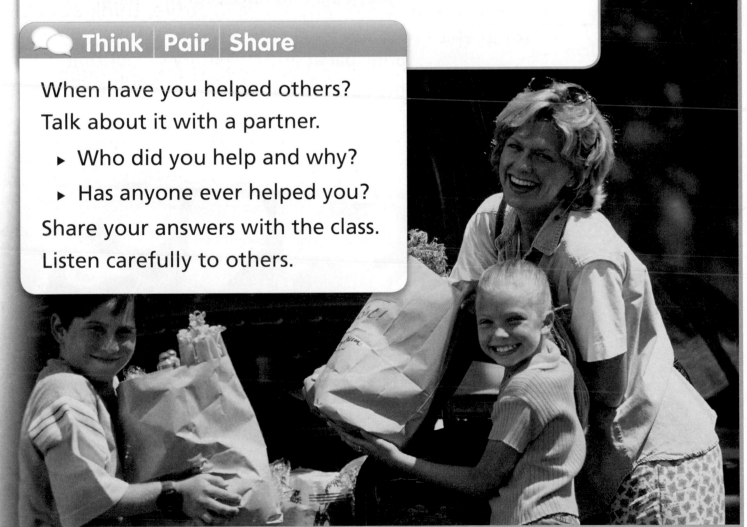

# ANCHOR TEXT

✓ **GENRE**

**Realistic fiction** is a story that could happen in real life. As you read, look for:

▶ characters who act like real people

▶ a setting that could be a real place

**MEET THE AUTHOR AND ILLUSTRATOR**

## Maryann Cocca-Leffler

Many of Maryann Cocca-Leffler's books are based on her own life. *Clams All Year* is about the time she went clam digging with her grandpa following a big storm. She wrote *Jack's Talent* after a boy said during a school visit that he had no talent for anything. The tie-loving Mr. Tanen was the principal at an elementary school that the author's two daughters attended.

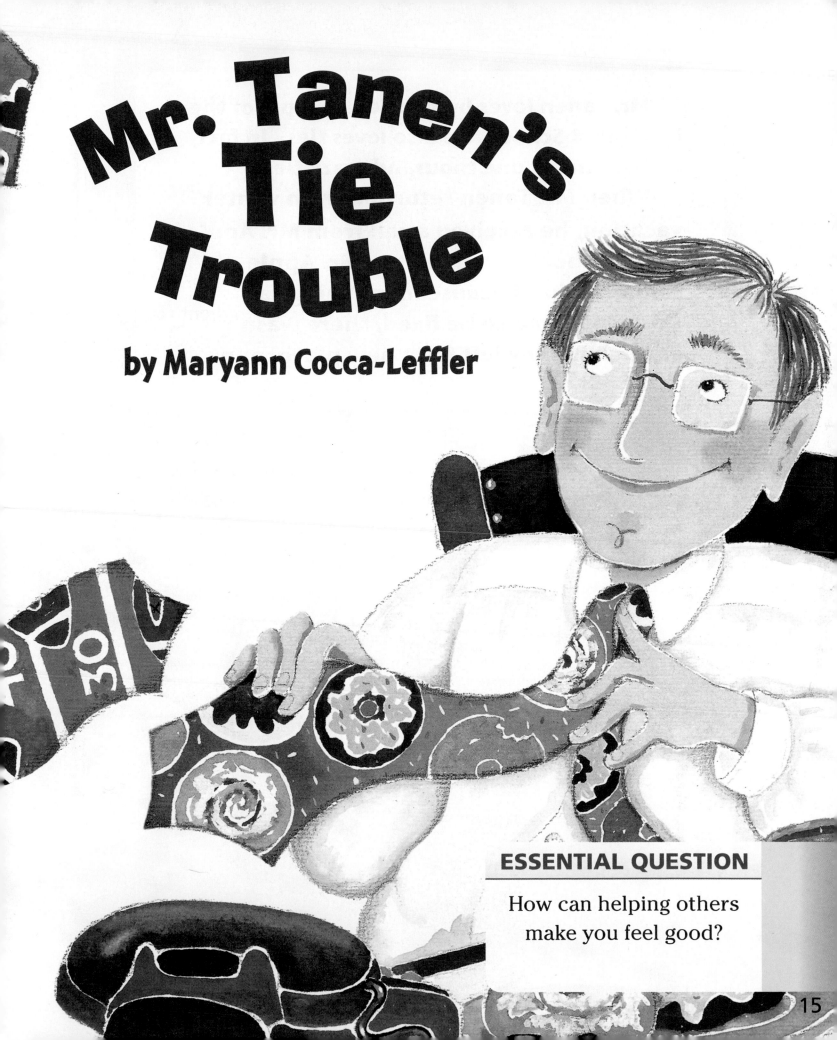

# Mr. Tanen's Tie Trouble

by Maryann Cocca-Leffler

**ESSENTIAL QUESTION**

How can helping others make you feel good?

Mr. Tanen loves being the principal of the Lynnhurst School. He also loves ties. In fact, he has almost one thousand crazy ties!

When Mr. Tanen returned from winter vacation, he received a call from Mr. Apple at the School Department. Mr. Apple told him that because many things at the school had to be fixed, there wasn't enough money left for a new playground.

Mr. Tanen sadly hung up the phone and gazed out at the broken-down playground. He heard a *clink-clank*. He looked up to see Kaylee and Alex lugging in a big jar filled with money.

"Here it is! $148.29 for the playground fund!" said Kaylee proudly.

"New playground, here we come!" cheered Alex.

Mr. Tanen didn't know what to say.

After school, Mr. Tanen sat in his office staring at the jar. He sighed. "Now I'm in a real pickle! This is not enough money for a playground. The kids will be so disappointed."

Mr. Apple's words floated around in his head:

"The playground will have to wait."

"You'll think of something."

"I wish our account was as full as your tie closet."

"Hmm . . . as full as my tie closet!" repeated Mr. Tanen.

PLAYGROUND
$ $ $
$ $ $

He jumped up, opened his closet, and shouted, "That's IT!  MY TIES!  Lynnhurst School WILL have a new playground!"

The next day, the entire town was plastered with signs.

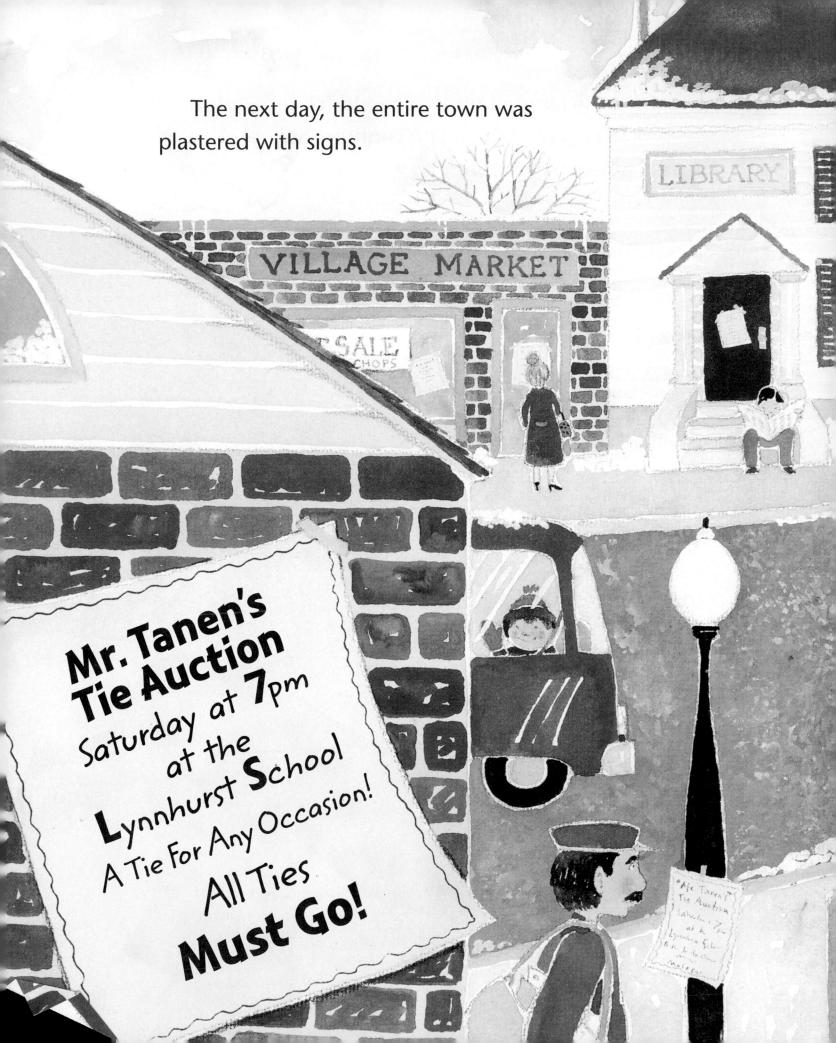

**Mr. Tanen's
Tie Auction**
Saturday at **7**pm
at the
**L**ynnhurst **S**chool
A Tie For Any Occasion!
All Ties
**Must Go!**

**ANALYZE THE TEXT**

**Understanding Characters** What does Mr. Tanen do to help raise money for the playground? What do his actions tell you about him?

21

Mrs. Sweet Apple noticed the sign on the grocery store window. She called her husband, Mr. Apple.

"Why is Mr. Tanen selling all his ties? Has he gone crazy?"

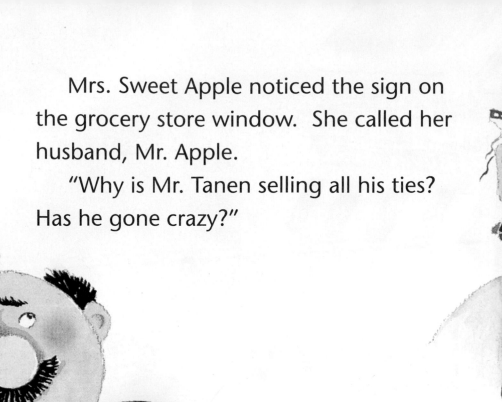

Mr. Apple told her about the school budget and the playground money. The town was buzzing all day . . .

Mrs. Sweet Apple called Monsieur Bijou at the bakery,

who called Cleo at
the cleaners,

who called Dr. Demi
the dentist . . .

It went on and on, until even
Zack, the night watchman at the
zoo, got the word:

## "Mr. Tanen is selling his ties!"

On Saturday, the whole town showed up for the auction. Monsieur Bijou started the bidding. "I'll give you $50 for the Doughnut and Danish Tie!"

Lolly the librarian bought the Book Tie.

Dr. Demi was the proud owner of the Toothbrush Tie.

Kaylee handed over her entire piggy bank for the Hot Dog Tie.

Mrs. Sweet Apple just had to have the Wedding Bells Tie, and of course, Mr. Apple chuckled as he paid quite a bit of cash for the Crabapple Tie.

* Mr. Tanen's *
Tie Auction
Saturday at 7pm
at the
Lynnhurst School
A Tie For My Grissel
All Ties
MUST GO!

The auction was a huge success!  Every tie was sold, except one.  Mr. Tanen couldn't part with his beloved Blue Ribbon Tie.  It was a present from Mr. Apple for being a great principal.  He looked out at a sea of townspeople, all wearing his ties.

"Thank you all. I have always taught my students, 'The more you give, the more you get.' With this money, the Lynnhurst School will have a new playground!"

Mr. Tanen swallowed hard. "My ties now belong to the town. Wear them proudly."

And throughout the spring,
that's just what everyone did.

But sometimes Mr. Tanen would forget his closet was empty. He would open it to get a tie, and with a tinge of sadness, he would remember. He only had one tie—and he was wearing it. Then he'd look outside at the playground being built. "You have to give to get," he thought.

Soon it was Opening Day at the new playground. Mr. Tanen had invited the whole town to the ribbon-cutting ceremony. He tucked his speech in his pocket, grabbed his special scissors, and adjusted his tie. He wished he had on his official Ribbon-Cutting Tie.

The schoolyard was overflowing with people. Mr. Tanen made his way through the crowd.

Then he saw it!

Mr. Tanen's Playground

The playground was tied in a giant ribbon
made from Mr. Tanen's ties!

Mrs. Sweet Apple and Mr. Apple were at the microphone.

"Mr. Tanen, you have taught us all, 'The more you give, the more you get,'" said Mrs. Sweet Apple. "You have given us a playground. We are giving you back your ties."

With that, Mr. Apple untied
the tie ribbon and announced:
"Mr. Tanen's Playground is

**NOW OPEN!"**

33

Mr. Tanen and his ties were
together again!

He slipped on his Swing and Slide
Tie and smiled.

**ANALYZE THE TEXT**

**Story Structure** What problem
does Mr. Tanen have after he sells
his ties? How does the ending solve
Mr. Tanen's problem?

# Dig Deeper

## Use Clues to Analyze the Text

Use these pages to learn about Story Structure and Understanding Characters.  Then read *Mr. Tanen's Tie Trouble* again.  Use what you learn to understand it better.

## Story Structure

In *Mr. Tanen's Tie Trouble*, you read a story about a principal who has to solve a problem. Who are the characters?  Where does the story take place?

Think about how the beginning of the story tells the problem that the characters have.  How is the problem solved at the end?  Use a story map to help you describe the **characters, setting,** and **plot** of *Mr. Tanen's Tie Trouble*.

| Characters | Setting |
|------------|---------|
| **Plot** ||

# Understanding Characters

The way that **characters** act when they have a problem tells you more about them. Think about how the people in the town try to help Mr. Tanen and the school. Many people come to the auction and buy Mr. Tanen's ties. This text evidence shows that they want to help raise money for the playground. Understanding how characters think, act, and feel helps you to better understand why things happen in the story.

# Your Turn

**How can helping others make you feel good?** Talk with a partner. Use text evidence from *Mr. Tanen's Tie Trouble* to tell your ideas. Also talk about times that you have helped others. Take turns listening and speaking. Use respectful ways to take your turn speaking.

## Classroom Conversation

Now talk about these questions with the class.

1. What decision do the characters make that helps Mr. Tanen solve his problem?

2. Why do the people in the town give Mr. Tanen his ties back?

3. How does Mr. Tanen feel when the people in the town give him back his ties? How do you know?

### WRITE ABOUT READING

**Response** How do you think the people in the town feel about Mr. Tanen? Write a few sentences to explain your ideas. Use the words and pictures in the story as text evidence to support your opinion.

### Writing Tip

Remember to start each proper noun with a capital letter.

# INFORMATIONAL TEXT

**The Jefferson Daily News**

✓ **GENRE**

**Informational text** gives facts about a topic.

✓ **TEXT FOCUS**

A **caption** tells more about a photo.

# The Jefferson Daily News

November 5

## Club Helps in Many Ways

by Ben Watts

The Helping Hands Club is one of the best clubs at Jefferson Elementary School. The children in this club volunteer their time to help other people and the community. Last month they gathered items to recycle from home and school. Many items, such as water bottles and juice containers, were placed in recycle bins. Some other items were used in the art classroom.

The club's sponsor, Mrs. Waters, was proud of all who helped. "Students created beautiful artwork from cloth and paper scraps. The club's hard work gave these items a new purpose," she said.

**Art made from scraps**

The Helping Hands Club has done many more things to help the community. They cleaned up the park and playground and collected food for the food bank. They had a bake sale to raise money for the animal shelter. Club members even decorated posters for bike safety week.

Malik is one of the members of the club. He told how the club helped someone he knew. "The Helping Hands Club helped my neighbor, Mrs. Dodge," he said. "She is 80 years old and lives alone. Our parents brought her hot food, and we pulled weeds in her yard. She was so happy and thankful, and she gave us all lemonade. Helping her made me feel happy, too!"

**The club holds a bake sale to help animals.**

**The club helps to clean up the park.**

The Helping Hands Club would like to invite you to a meeting. You can find out what the club is all about and how you can participate. You can even share your own ideas! "This club helps in many ways," said Principal Ramirez. "It is a great club to join!"

**Principal Ramirez tells about the club.**

# What:

Helping Hands Club Meeting

# When:

December 1

# Time:

3:30 p.m.

# Where:

Mrs. Waters's classroom,

Room 107

# Compare Texts

## TEXT TO TEXT

**Compare and Contrast** Imagine that Mr. Tanen is the principal at Jefferson Elementary School. Would he think that the Helping Hands Club is a good club to join? Explain your thoughts to a partner. Use text evidence from both selections to help you answer.

## TEXT TO SELF

**Write a Description** Which of Mr. Tanen's ties do you like the best? Write a few sentences describing the tie you like. Then tell when a person might wear the tie.

## TEXT TO WORLD

**Connect to Science** Think about what you might see, hear, or feel at Mr. Tanen's playground. Write a poem about it. Use describing words.

ELA RL.2.1, RL.2.7, W.2.8

# Grammar

**Pronouns**  A **pronoun** can take the place of a noun. To replace a **noun** that is the subject of a sentence, use the pronoun *I, he, she, it, we,* or *they.*  To replace a noun that comes after a **verb,** use the pronoun *me, him, her, it, us,* or *them.*  **Reflexive pronouns,** such as *myself, himself, herself, themselves,* and *ourselves,* are also used after verbs.

| Nouns | Pronouns |
|---|---|
| The children want a new playground. | They want a new playground. |
| Mr. Tanen likes ties. | He likes ties. |
| My mother helped the principal. | My mother helped him. |
| Our family bought ties for our family. | Our family bought ties for ourselves. |

**Try This!** **Name the pronouns that can replace the underlined words.  Then rewrite the sentences using the pronouns.**

❶ Lou and Kim sat on the swings.

❷ I like the slide.

❸ My brother plays by my brother in the sand.

ELA L.2.1c

When you write, try not to use the same nouns over and over again. Use pronouns or reflexive pronouns to take the place of repeated nouns. This will make your writing better.

| Sentences with Repeated Subjects | Better Sentences |
|---|---|
| The two girls counted the money. The two girls hoped they had raised enough. | The two girls counted the money. They hoped they had raised enough. |

## Connect Grammar to Writing

**When you revise your story paragraph, look for repeated nouns. Use pronouns to take their place.**

# Narrative Writing

**✓ Elaboration** Use details when you write a **story.**
Details help your reader picture what the story is about.

Ahmed drafted a one-paragraph story about a little
boy who helped his mother. Later, he added some
details to make his story more interesting.

## Writing Checklist

☑ **Organization**
Did I include a
beginning, a middle,
and an end?

☑ **Development**
Do my words tell
what the characters
are feeling?

☑ **Elaboration**
Did I add details to
tell the reader
more?

☑ **Conventions**
Did I use spelling
patterns to help me
spell words?

## Revised Draft

Omar wanted to help his
She had been sick for a week.
mother.∧He came home early
playing with his friends in
one day from∧the park. His
kitchen
mother was sitting at the table.
∧

He wanted to do something to

help. First, he began to rinse

the dishes.

ELA W.2.3, W.2.5, L.2.2d

# Omar's Gift

## by Ahmed Hakin

Omar wanted to help his mother. She had been sick for a week. He came home early one day from playing with his friends in the park. His mother was sitting at the kitchen table. He wanted to do something to help. First, he began to rinse the dishes. After that, he put them in the dishwasher. His mother looked at him and said, "You are a good son, Omar." She smiled at him. Omar knew that he had just given his mother a gift. It was a gift that made them both happy.

## Reading as a Writer

How do the details that Ahmed added tell his readers more? Where can you add details to your story?

I added details to my final paper to make it more interesting.

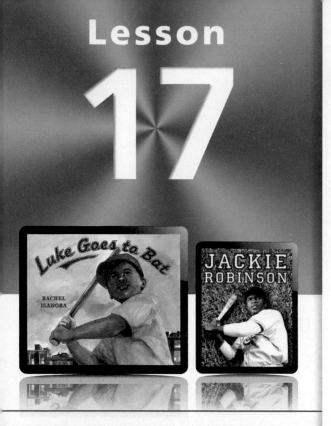

Luke Goes to Bat
RACHEL ISADORA

JACKIE ROBINSON

**Q LANGUAGE DETECTIVE**

**Talk About Words**
Work with a partner.
Choose two Vocabulary
words. Use them in
the same sentence.
Share your sentences
with the class.

# Vocabulary in Context

▶ Read each **Context Card**.

▶ Make up a new sentence that uses a Vocabulary word.

**1   practice**

If you practice hitting the baseball every day, your hitting will get better.

**2   hurried**

The soccer player hurried to stop the ball. He moved fast.

### 3  position

The batter is in position to hit the baseball.

### 4  roared

The crowd roared loudly as the player caught the ball.

### 5  extra

The extra players for the football team sat on the bench.

### 6  curb

After skating, the girl rested on the curb outside her house.

### 7  cheered

The audience clapped and cheered as the player scored a goal.

### 8  final

When the game ended, the final score was four to two.

# Read and Comprehend

**Sequence of Events** In *Luke Goes to Bat*, the author tells about Luke and the things that happen to him one summer. The order in which events happen is called the **sequence of events**. Putting these events in order in a chart like the one below can help you understand the story.

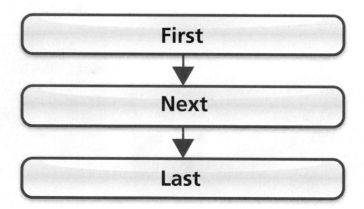

First

↓

Next

↓

Last

☑ **TARGET STRATEGY**

**Visualize** As you read, use text evidence to picture what is happening. This will help you understand and remember important ideas and details.

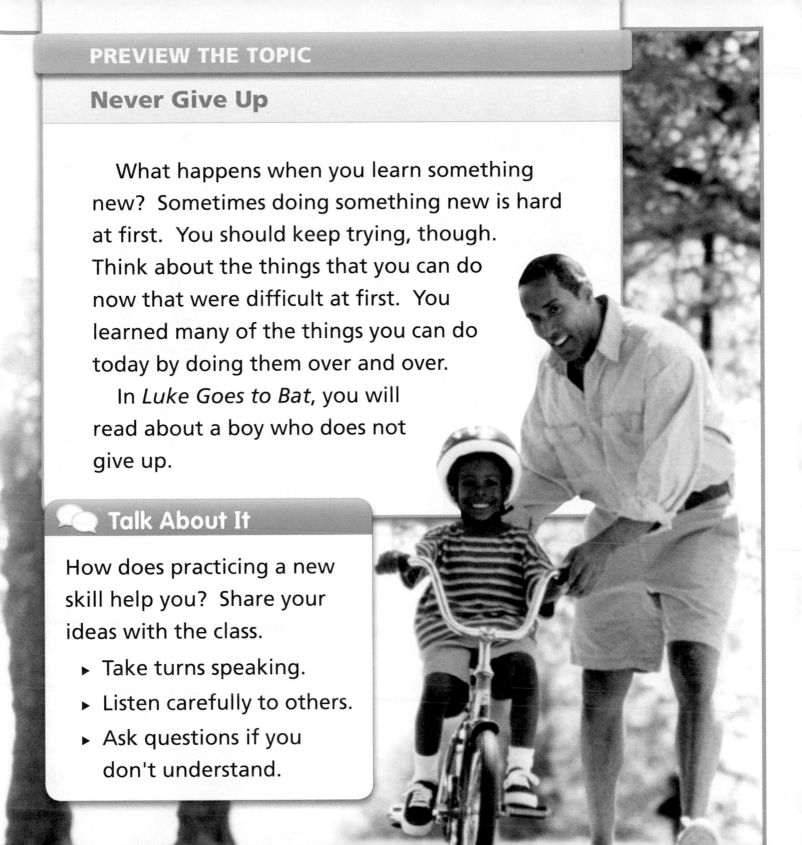

## Never Give Up

What happens when you learn something new? Sometimes doing something new is hard at first. You should keep trying, though. Think about the things that you can do now that were difficult at first. You learned many of the things you can do today by doing them over and over.

In *Luke Goes to Bat*, you will read about a boy who does not give up.

### 💬 Talk About It

How does practicing a new skill help you? Share your ideas with the class.

▶ Take turns speaking.

▶ Listen carefully to others.

▶ Ask questions if you don't understand.

Luke Goes to Bat

RACHEL ISADORA

✅ **GENRE**

**Realistic fiction** is a story that could happen in real life. As you read, look for:

▸ characters who act like real people

▸ a setting that could be a real place

**MEET THE AUTHOR AND ILLUSTRATOR**

# Rachel Isadora

Rachel Isadora grew up wanting to be a ballerina. She was so shy that she wouldn't dance in front of her class until she had practiced the steps in an empty room. Later, she injured her foot and couldn't dance anymore.

She decided to become an artist instead. Today, Ms. Isadora writes and illustrates children's books about ballet, music, and baseball.

# LUKE GOES TO BAT

by Rachel Isadora

It was Brooklyn. It was summer.
It was baseball. All day long the kids on
Bedford Avenue played stickball in the
streets. Except for Luke.

"When you're older," his big brother, Nicky, told him.

"He's just a squirt," one of the other kids said, laughing.

So Luke watched the games from the curb, and then he'd practice.

He threw a ball against the wall next to the deli. He practiced his swing over and over again. He ran as fast as he could up and down the block.

He wanted to be ready when it was time.

And at night, whenever the Dodgers were playing, Luke hurried up to the roof, where he could see the lights of Ebbets Field. When he heard the crowd go wild, he imagined his favorite player, Jackie Robinson, had hit a home run.

Someday, Luke thought, I will hit a home run, too.

Finally, one morning, the team was short a player.

"Franky had to go to his aunt's!"

"Who we gonna get?"

"Hey," said Luke, "what about me?"

Everyone was quiet.

"Aw, come on," said his brother.
"Give him a chance."

"We got nobody else."

"He better not mess up."

They put him in left field. No balls came his way,
so he just stood there.

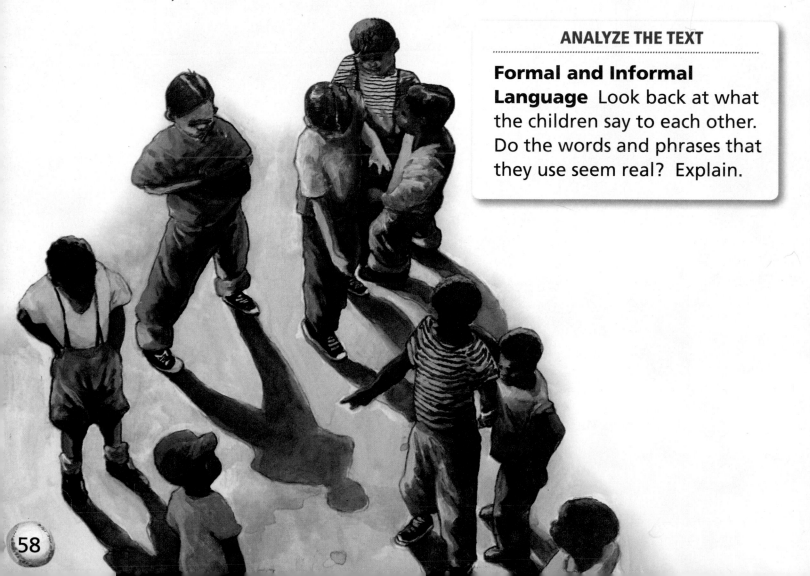

**ANALYZE THE TEXT**

**Formal and Informal Language** Look back at what the children say to each other. Do the words and phrases that they use seem real? Explain.

When it was his turn up at bat, Luke took a
few practice swings, then stepped up to the plate.

"I'll show them," Luke muttered.

The ball whizzed past.

"Strike one!"

Luke held the bat higher.

"Strike two!"

Luke was barely in position when the next
ball flew past and the catcher yelled, "Out!"

"You stink," Luke heard.

He got up to bat one more time but struck out again.

"Sometimes it just goes that way," his brother told him.

Franky came back in the afternoon, so Luke spent the rest of the day on the curb. He was sure they'd never let him play again.

Grandma was in the kitchen when he got home.

"I finally got a chance to play with the team," Luke told her.

Grandma could tell that the game hadn't gone well. "Not everyone plays like Jackie Robinson all the time," she said. "Not even Jackie Robinson."

Luke didn't smile.

"By the way," Grandma said, "are you doing anything tomorrow night?"

Luke shrugged.

"Well, if you're so busy, someone else will have to go with me to the game at Ebbets Field."

"What? You mean a real game?"

Grandma held up two tickets.

Ebbets Field was ablaze with lights. But this time, Luke didn't have to imagine the game.

"Thanks for taking me, Grandma," he said.

They watched the Dodgers and Phillies battle it out. The game went into extra innings. By the time the Dodgers got up to bat in the bottom of the fourteenth inning, the score was still tied, 8–8. With two outs, Jackie Robinson was up.

The crowd roared.

"Come on, Jackie!" Luke yelled.

The pitcher threw a curveball. Jackie swung.

"Strike one!" the umpire called.

The pitcher wound up. He threw a fastball and
Jackie missed.

"Strike two!"

Three balls followed.

All eyes at Ebbets Field rested on Jackie. The Dodgers
could still win.

Luke shouted with the crowd. "Give it to 'em, Jackie!
You show 'em!"

Jackie looked around from under his cap, then dug his
feet into the dirt.

The pitcher began his windup. "You can do it, Jackie,"
Luke whispered. "You can do it."

Suddenly, Luke heard the loud crack of a bat. When he looked up, the ball was flying over his head, flying over the scoreboard, flying over the walls of Ebbets Field! The crowd went wild!

Luke stood up on his seat and cheered, "You showed 'em, Jackie!"

"What a game!" Grandma said. "See, you can't give up. Even Jackie Robinson's got to keep trying."

Luke didn't answer.

When Luke got home, he ran up to the roof. The lights were going out at Ebbets Field.

"Come on down! It's bedtime!" Nicky called.

Just then, Luke saw a ball lying on the ground.

"Look!" he said, picking it up. "This is the home run ball that Jackie Robinson hit tonight!"

"Naw. That's just some old ball a kid hit up on the roof," Nick said, laughing, as he went downstairs.

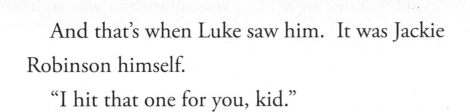

And that's when Luke saw him. It was Jackie Robinson himself.

"I hit that one for you, kid."

Before Luke could say a word, Jackie ran to the dugout to join the other Dodgers. But he looked back one more time.

"Hey, kid," he said. "Your grandma was right.
You can't give up."

"Thanks, Mr. Robinson."

The final lights went out at Ebbets Field. Luke
looked down at the winning ball and smiled.

"I won't," he whispered to himself.

And he didn't.

**ANALYZE THE TEXT**

**Sequence of Events** Think about the story's events. What lesson does Luke learn?

# Dig Deeper

## Use Clues to Analyze the Text

Use these pages to learn about Sequence of Events and Formal and Informal Language. Then read *Luke Goes to Bat* again. Use what you learn to understand it better.

## Sequence of Events

*Luke Goes to Bat* is about events that happen to a boy named Luke. The events in the story happen in order. Knowing the **sequence of events** can help you understand the story.

As you read, think about what happens and what the characters learn from the events. Then think about the lesson that you can learn. You can use a chart like the one below to show the order of events.

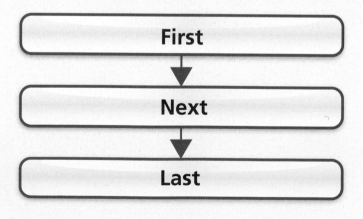

First

↓

Next

↓

Last

# Formal and Informal Language

Authors write **dialogue** to show what characters say. Sometimes the way a character speaks is **formal,** or follows correct grammar rules. Sometimes it is **informal,** or more relaxed. In *Luke Goes to Bat*, the boys sometimes use informal language as they talk to each other. An author uses formal and informal language to make what the characters say seem real.

# Your Turn

 **Why is it important to keep trying even if something is difficult to do?** Take turns sharing your ideas. Use text evidence from *Luke Goes to Bat* to support what you say. Ask questions if you need more information about what your partner says.

 **Classroom Conversation**

Now talk about these questions with the class.

1. What lesson does Luke learn?

2. How does it help Luke to see Jackie Robinson almost strike out?

3. What might happen the next time Luke plays baseball with his friends? Use text evidence to explain your answer.

## WRITE ABOUT READING

my
WriteSmart

**Response** Look back at pages 66–71. How do the pictures show you what is real and what Luke is imagining? Does this help you understand the story? Write a paragraph to explain what you think.

### Writing Tip

Remember that a pronoun can take the place of a noun. Use a pronoun instead of using the same noun over and over.

# INFORMATIONAL TEXT

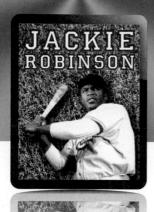

☑ **GENRE**

**Informational text** gives facts about a topic. This is a website.

☑ **TEXT FOCUS**

A **website** is an online collection of pages about a topic. As you read, pay attention to how the website looks. Which parts would help you move to another part of the website?

File    Edit    View    Favorites

# JACKIE ROBINSON

### Young Jackie

Jackie Roosevelt Robinson was born on January 31, 1919, in Cairo, Georgia. He and his family soon moved to Pasadena, California.

Jackie was good at sports, even as a young boy. He loved to run, play, and have fun with his friends.

Jackie was the youngest child in a family of athletes.

## Jackie Grows Up

In high school and college, Jackie didn't sit on the curb and watch others play sports. He would practice a lot. Jackie was good at football, baseball, basketball, and track. Fans cheered for him when he played.

## Into the Major League

In 1947, Jackie became the first African American to play Major League Baseball. Before that time, African Americans were not allowed to play in the major leagues.

Jackie played for the Brooklyn Dodgers. The position he played was second base. Fans would stay to watch him if a game went into extra innings. They roared when the team won.

Jackie was famous for stealing bases. In this photo, he hurried to get to home plate.

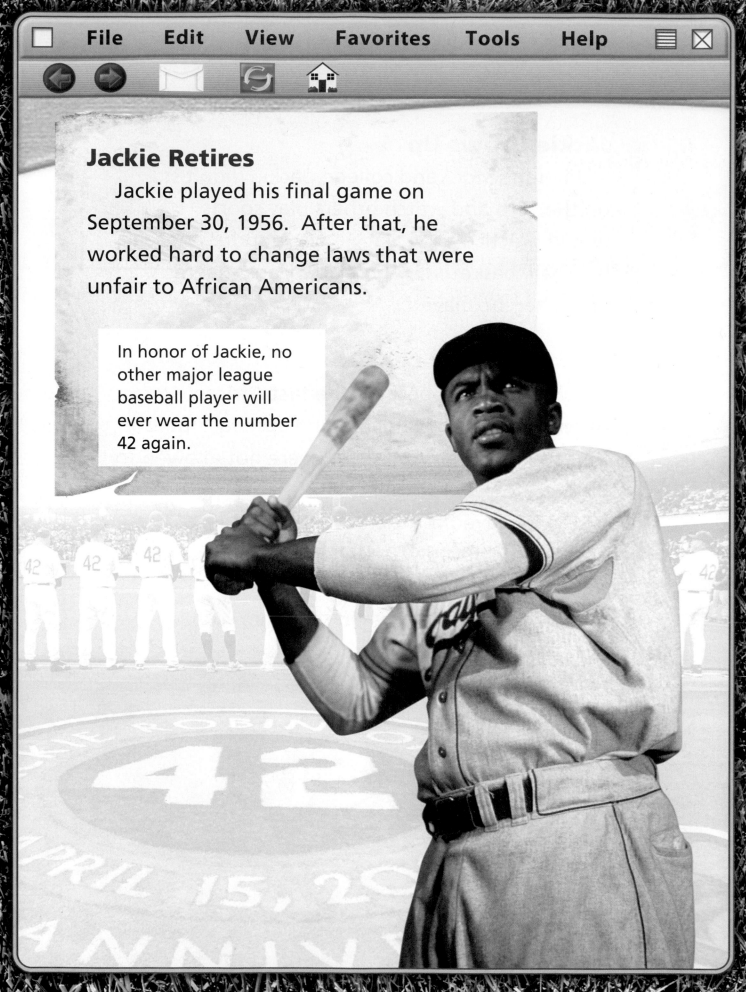

## Jackie Retires

Jackie played his final game on September 30, 1956. After that, he worked hard to change laws that were unfair to African Americans.

In honor of Jackie, no other major league baseball player will ever wear the number 42 again.

# Compare Texts

## TEXT TO TEXT

**Share Differences** Think about why the authors wrote *Luke Goes to Bat* and *Jackie Robinson*. How is the author's purpose for writing the story different from the author's purpose for making the website? Share your ideas with a partner.

## TEXT TO SELF

**Write a Story** Have you ever worked hard to get good at something the way Luke did? Write sentences about your experience.

## TEXT TO WORLD

**Connect to Technology** Luke watched baseball at Ebbets Field. How might seeing a game in person be different from seeing it on television? Share your opinion with a partner.

**ELA** RI.2.6, W.2.3, W.2.8

# Grammar

**Digital Resources**

► Multimedia Grammar Glossary

► GrammarSnap Video

**Pronouns and Verbs** A **verb** can name an action that is happening now. A **pronoun** can tell who or what is doing the action. If the pronoun *he*, *she*, or *it* comes before a verb that tells about now, add *-s* or *-es* to the verb. If the pronoun *we, I,* or *they* comes before a verb that tells about now, do not add *-s* or *-es*.

| Add *-s* or *-es* to Verb | No Change to Verb |
|---|---|
| He hits the ball. <br> She catches the ball. <br> It breaks the window. | We hit the ball. <br> I catch the ball. <br> They break the window. |

**Try This!** **Choose the correct verb to complete each sentence. Then write the sentence correctly.**

1 We (watch, watches) the game.

2 She (play, plays) well.

3 They (buy, buys) new bats.

4 It (roll, rolls) toward second base.

Edit your writing carefully. Make sure the verbs that go with the pronouns have the correct endings.

| Singular Pronoun and Verb | Plural Pronoun and Verb |
|---|---|
| He looks at the ticket. She pitches to the batter. | We walk to the seats. They watch the game together. |

## Connect Grammar to Writing

When you edit your story paragraph, be sure you have written the correct verb to go with each pronoun.

# Narrative Writing ✔my WriteSmart

✔**Development** Dialogue is what the characters say in a **story.** Dialogue can show what your characters are like.

Nick drafted a story about a girl who meets her favorite writer. Later, he added dialogue to show how his characters act and how they feel.

## Writing Checklist

✔ **Organization**
Do things happen in a way that makes sense?

✔ **Development**
Did I use dialogue to tell what the characters are like?

✔ **Elaboration**
Do the words I chose show how the characters feel?

✔ **Conventions**
Did I use different types of sentences?

### Revised Draft

"There he is! " Tonya shouted.
ᴧ Today, Tonya was going to

meet her hero. Shane Jonas

was signing his books at the

bookstore. Shane wrote stories

about Tik and Tak. Tonya had

read them all.
"Hi," Shane said as
ᴧ Tonya and her dad walked
     "What's your name? " Then he
up to the table. ~~Shane Jonas~~
                              ᴧ

reached out to shake her hand.

ELA W.2.3, W.2.5

# Tonya and Her Hero
## by Nick Haswell

"There he is!" Tonya shouted. Today, Tonya was going to meet her hero. Shane Jonas was signing his books at the bookstore. Shane wrote stories about Tik and Tak. Tonya had read them all.

"Hi," Shane said as Tonya and her dad walked up to the table. "What's your name?" Then he reached out to shake her hand.

"I'm Tonya, and this is my dad," Tonya said. "I love your books!"

"I love to hear that," Shane replied. After that he smiled and wrote a long note in her book.

## Reading as a Writer

How does dialogue show more about the characters? Where can you add dialogue in your story?

I added dialogue to tell more about what my characters are like.

85

**My Name is \* Me llamo**
**Gabriela**

**Poems About Reading and Writing**

---

**Q LANGUAGE DETECTIVE**

**Talk About Words** A verb's tense tells if something happened in the past, is happening now, or will happen in the future. Work with a partner. Find the Vocabulary words that are verbs. Then say the sentence again with the verb in a different tense.

# Vocabulary in Context

▶ **Read each Context Card.**

▶ **Talk about a picture. Use a different Vocabulary word from the one in the card.**

**1**

### accepted

The student gave the teacher an apple. She accepted it.

**2**

### express

You can express your ideas by writing a story.

### 3 taught

This teacher taught his class a new word.

### 4 grand

A grand award is a top prize in a contest.

### 5 pretend

This girl is not a real doctor. She is a pretend doctor.

### 6 prize

The best speller received first prize in the spelling bee.

### 7 wonder

The children wonder when the caterpillar will become a butterfly.

### 8 fluttering

The butterfly is fluttering its wings as it flies. The wings move quickly.

# Read and Comprehend

**TARGET SKILL**

**Understanding Characters** *My Name Is Gabriela* is a true story that tells about the poet Gabriela Mistral. Pay attention to what Gabriela says and does. Use these clues and other text evidence to understand Gabriela and why the author wrote about her. You can write details in a chart like this.

| Character | Words, Thoughts, Actions | Trait |
|-----------|--------------------------|-------|
|           |                          |       |

**TARGET STRATEGY**

**Analyze/Evaluate** To **analyze** as you read, think about the author's words and story events. Then **evaluate,** or decide, how the words and events help you understand what is important in the text.

## Reading and Writing

People have been reading and writing for thousands of years. Writing is a way to record information. We can still read things that were written long ago. Some of your favorite books might be very old. Some day in the future, people may read what you write today!

In *My Name Is Gabriela*, you will read about Gabriela Mistral. She was a poet who knew that reading and writing are important.

### 💬 Think | Write | Pair | Share

How do you feel about reading and writing poetry? Make a list of words that describe your feelings. Share your list with a partner. Take turns speaking. Do you have any words that are the same? Share your list with the class.

# ANCHOR TEXT

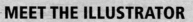

My Name is * Me llamo
Gabriela

The Life of * la vida de
Gabriela Mistral

## ✅ GENRE

A **biography** tells about events in a person's life. As you read, look for:

▸ information about why a person is important
▸ events in time order

**MEET THE AUTHOR**

## Monica Brown

Monica Brown's daughters think it's pretty cool to have a mom who's an author. At book signings, "They'll walk up and announce that it was their Mommy who wrote this book," Ms. Brown says. The family lives in Arizona, not far from the Grand Canyon.

**MEET THE ILLUSTRATOR**

## John Parra

John Parra grew up in California in a home filled with Mexican art, food, and traditions. Today, Mr. Parra's colorful artwork can be seen in galleries, on posters and CD covers, and in the pages of children's books.

# My Name is
# Gabriela

by Monica Brown   illustrated by John Parra

**ESSENTIAL QUESTION**

Why are reading and
writing important?

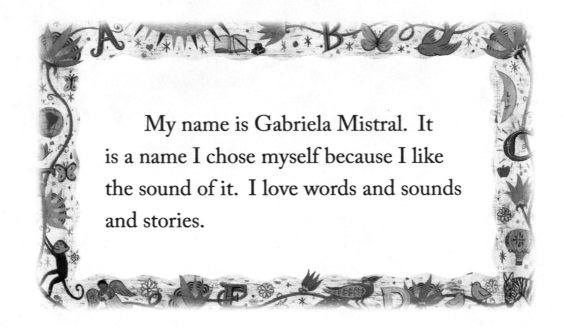

My name is Gabriela Mistral. It is a name I chose myself because I like the sound of it. I love words and sounds and stories.

GABRIELA MISTRAL

93

When I was a little girl, I lived with my mother and Emelina, my sister, in a small house in the beautiful Elqui Valley in Chile. From my bedroom window I could see the Andes Mountains.

When I couldn't sleep I would look up at the mountains and wonder what could be beyond them. Zebras with polka dots? Rainbow-colored flowers? Angels reading books?

I loved words—I liked the sounds they made rolling

off my tongue and I liked the

way they could express how I felt.

When I saw a butterfly fluttering, I noticed the way

the words fluttering butterfly sounded together—like a poem.

I taught myself to read so that I could read other people's words and stories. I read stories about princes and princesses, about monsters, and about birds and flowers.

**ANALYZE THE TEXT**

**Author's Word Choice**
What words does the author use to tell how Gabriela feels about words?

I also liked to write poems, sing songs, and tell stories using the words that I knew. I told stories about happy times and sad times, about mothers and babies and little children.

I liked to play school with the children of my village.
I pretended to be the teacher, and my friends, Sofía, Ana,
and Pedro, were my pupils.

Pedro would always say that I was mean because I
made him write his ABCs until he knew all the letters
of the alphabet. But I told him that the alphabet is
important. How else would he create words and tell his
stories without it?

In our pretend class we sang songs like:

The baby chicks are saying,

Peep, peep, peep.

It means they're cold and hungry.

It means they need some sleep.

That was Sofía's favorite song. During recess we
had fun, running and chasing and laughing and playing.

When I grew up I became a real teacher and writer. I taught the children of Chile, and many of my students became teachers themselves.

I still wrote poems—happy poems, sad poems, stories of mothers and children. But I also wrote poems about animals—about parrots and peacocks and even rats!

**ANALYZE THE TEXT**

**Understanding Characters** What does the author want you to know about how Gabriela feels about teaching and learning? How do you know?

I also traveled to far away places. I never saw
zebras with polka dots or rainbow-colored flowers,
but I met wonderful children and their teachers.
I traveled to Europe—to France and Italy.

I traveled to Mexico.

I traveled to the United States.

Everywhere I went, I wrote and taught and met teachers. I saw how all over the world, people wanted their children to learn.

My stories traveled the world with me. People liked
to read my happy stories, my sad stories, my stories of
women and children, my stories of parrots and peacocks,
of old lions and of the fisherfolk, who slept in the sand
and dreamt of the sea.

NOBEL PRIZE

And because people from all over the world loved my stories so, I was given a very special prize—the Nobel Prize for Literature.

When I accepted the grand award, I thought of the beautiful mountains outside of my window in Chile, of my mother and sister, of the children of my village, and of all the stories that still need to be told.

# Dig Deeper

## Use Clues to Analyze the Text

Use these pages to learn about Understanding Characters and Author's Word Choice. Then read *My Name Is Gabriela* again. Use what you learn to understand it better.

## Understanding Characters

*My Name Is Gabriela* is a biography that tells about a poet named Gabriela. In a biography, the author gives details to help the reader understand what the person is like. You can use a chart like the one below to show details about Gabriela. The text evidence you write can help you figure out why she is important.

| Character | Words, Thoughts, Actions | Trait |
|-----------|--------------------------|-------|
|           |                          |       |

# Author's Word Choice

An author chooses strong words to help tell about places, characters, and things. Words and phrases can help the reader picture what the author is telling about. For example, an author might use the words *tiny* and *colorful* to tell about a butterfly. As you read, look for words that tell how things look, feel, and sound.

# Your Turn

 **Why are reading and writing important?** Talk to a partner about your ideas. Look back at *My Name Is Gabriela* for text evidence to support what you say. Be sure to ask questions if you need more information about what your partner says.

## 💬 Classroom Conversation

Now talk about these questions with the class.

1. What events in this biography explain how Gabriela became important?

2. How did Gabriela get ideas for her stories?

3. Why do you think the author wrote about Gabriela? Use text evidence to help you answer.

## WRITE ABOUT READING ⋯⋯⋯⋯⋯⋯⋯

**Response** How would you describe Gabriela?
Write a paragraph telling what she is like.
Use text evidence from the words and
pictures to help you.

### Writing Tip

Make sure that each sentence
has a verb with the correct
ending to match its subject.

# POETRY

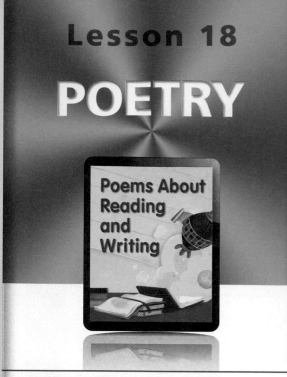

Poems About Reading and Writing

☑ **GENRE**

**Poetry** uses the sound of words to show pictures and feelings.

☑ **TEXT FOCUS**

**Rhythm** is a pattern of beats, like music. The words and phrases in poetry can give it rhythm and meaning.

# Poems About Reading and Writing

When you read a poem, do you pretend to be in the poem? When you write a poem, do you express wonder about things? These poems are about reading and writing.

## Share the Adventure

Pages and pages
A seesaw of ideas—
Share the adventure

Fiction, nonfiction:
Door to our past and future
Swinging back and forth

WHAM! The book slams shut,
But we read it together
With our minds open

*by Patricia and*
*Fredrick McKissack*

# The Period

Fat little period, round as a ball,
You'd think it would roll,
But it doesn't
At all.
Where it stops,
There it plops,
There it stubbornly stays,
At the end of a sentence
For days and days.

"Get out of my way!"
Cries the sentence. "Beware!"
But the period seems not to hear
   or to care.
Like a stone in the road,
It won't budge, it won't bend.
If it spoke, it would say to a sentence,
## "The end."

*by Richard Armour*

# Keep a Poem in Your Pocket

Keep a poem in your pocket
and a picture in your head
and you'll never feel lonely
at night when you're in bed.

The little poem will sing to you
the little picture bring to you
a dozen dreams to dance to you
at night when you're in bed.

So—
Keep a picture in your pocket
and a poem in your head
and you'll never feel lonely
at night when you're in bed.

*by Beatrice Schenk de Regniers*

## Write a Poem

Write a poem about your favorite book.
Think about how you can use rhythm, rhyme,
and repetition to make your poem fun to read.
Share your poem with a partner. Talk about
how the words add rhythm and meaning.

# Compare Texts

## TEXT TO TEXT

**Connect to Poetry** Gabriela Mistral loved to read and write. Look back at the poems you just read. Which poem do you think Gabriela would have liked the best? Write a few sentences to give your opinion. Give reasons using text evidence from *My Name Is Gabriela.*

## TEXT TO SELF

**Tell a Story** How does Gabriela help people learn? How has a teacher made a difference in your life? Tell a partner. Use facts and details to tell what happened.

## TEXT TO WORLD

**Find Facts** Gabriela grew up in Chile. Use the index of a reference book to look up information about Chile. Make two fact cards with information you learned.

Chile is over 4,000 kilometers long from north to south.

ELA RI.2.5, W.2.1, SL.2.4

# Grammar

Digital Resources

▶ Multimedia
Grammar Glossary

**The Verb *be*** The **verbs** *am*, *is*, and *are* tell about something that is happening now. The verbs *was* and *were* tell about something that happened in the **past.** Use *am*, *is*, or *was* if the sentence tells about one noun. Use *are* or *were* if the sentence tells about more than one.

| Now | In the Past |
|---|---|
| I am tired. | I was awake last night. |
| Ann is a teacher. | Ann was a teacher last year, too. |
| The boys are in Chile. | The boys were in Mexico last week. |

**Try This!** **Choose the correct verb to complete each sentence. Then write the sentence correctly.**

1 Gabriela (is, are) famous.

2 Her students (was, were) grateful.

3 Her books (is, are) easy to find.

4 My grandfather (was, were) a big fan.

You can combine sentences that have the same subject and verb. This will make your writing smoother.

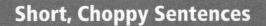
**Short, Choppy Sentences**

The boy is a good reader.

The boy is a good writer.

**Smoother Sentence**

The boy is a good reader and writer.

## Connect Grammar to Writing

**When you revise your paragraph that describes, try combining sentences with the same subject and verb.**

# Narrative Writing

**☑ Elaboration** You can use sense words to tell how things look, feel, smell, sound, and taste.

Alice wrote a draft of a **description.** She wanted to tell about her favorite place. Later, she added sense words to make her description come alive.

## Writing Checklist

**☑ Purpose**
Did I make the readers feel like they are there?

**☑ Organization**
Did I start by telling what I am describing?

**☑ Elaboration**
Did I use sense words to tell more?

**☑ Conventions**
Have I combined ideas and sentences when I can?

### Revised Draft

My family goes to Long

Beach almost every summer.

I love it at the beach. I
                    soft, hot
like walking on the ˄sand. I
                      pounding
love to listen to the ˄waves hit

the shore. The many smells
  spicy
of ˄food make me hungry. My
                    a big, cool
brother usually buys me ~~an~~ ˄ice
         It always tastes delicious!
cream cone.˄

# Our Summers at Long Beach
## by Alice O'Brien

My family goes to Long Beach almost every summer. I love it at the beach. I like walking on the soft, hot sand. I love to listen to the pounding waves hit the shore. The many smells of spicy food make me hungry. My brother usually buys me a big, cool ice cream cone. It always tastes delicious!

## Reading as a Writer

Which sense words did Alice add? What sense words can you add to your story?

I used sense words to tell the reader more about how things look, feel, smell, taste, and sound.

Q **LANGUAGE DETECTIVE**

**Talk About Words**
Work with a partner. Think about times when you might use each Vocabulary word in speaking or writing. Do you and your partner have similar ideas or different ideas?

# Vocabulary in Context

▶ Read each Context Card.

▶ Ask a question that uses one of the Vocabulary words.

---

**1** **assistant**

The assistant is helping to put up this sign.

---

**2** **agreed**

The people agreed that this road needed a stop sign.

### 3 polite

This sign reminds children to be polite, or nice, to others.

**PLEASE BE QUIET IN THE LIBRARY**

### 4 failed

The sign failed to keep the dog off the grass.

NO PETS ALLOWED

### 5 tearing

The worker is tearing apart this old sign.

### 6 wisdom

The words of wisdom on this billboard teach us to act the right way.

Be Safe! Drive Slowly.

### 7 cleared

The crossing guard cleared the way so these children could cross.

STOP

### 8 trouble

Without signs, drivers would have trouble knowing when to stop.

# Read and Comprehend

**Text and Graphic Features** Pictures in a story are kinds of **graphic features.** These features can help readers to better understand what they read.

As you read *The Signmaker's Assistant*, look carefully at the signs in the pictures. They can help you figure out what is happening in the story. A chart like the one below can help you keep track of what the pictures tell you.

| Picture | Page Number | Purpose |
|---------|-------------|---------|
|         |             |         |

**Question** Ask questions about what you are reading. Look for text evidence to answer your questions.

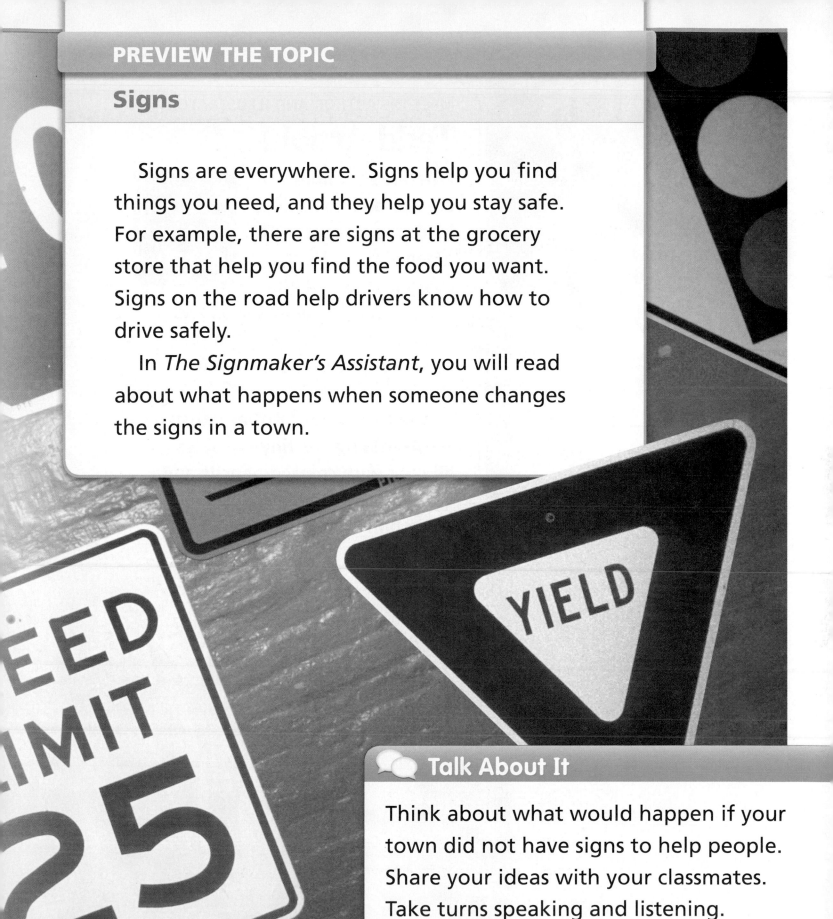

## Signs

Signs are everywhere. Signs help you find things you need, and they help you stay safe. For example, there are signs at the grocery store that help you find the food you want. Signs on the road help drivers know how to drive safely.

In *The Signmaker's Assistant*, you will read about what happens when someone changes the signs in a town.

### Talk About It

Think about what would happen if your town did not have signs to help people. Share your ideas with your classmates. Take turns speaking and listening. What did you learn from others?

# ANCHOR TEXT

## ☑ GENRE

**Humorous fiction** is a story that is written to make the reader laugh. As you read, look for:

▸ characters who do or say funny things

▸ events that would not happen in real life

**MEET THE AUTHOR AND ILLUSTRATOR**

# Tedd Arnold

When Tedd Arnold creates an illustration, he draws a scene with a pencil first. Next, using brown and blue watercolors, he paints shadows around the edges. He then paints lots of bright colors over the shadows.

The next step is rather unusual. Mr. Arnold makes tiny scribbles all over with colored pencils and outlines everything in black. It takes him two days to make each illustration.

# THE SIGNMAKER's ASSISTANT

by Tedd Arnold

Everyone in town agreed. The old signmaker did
the finest work for miles around. Under his brush
ordinary letters became beautiful words—words of
wisdom, words of warning, or words that simply said
which door to use.

When he painted STOP, people stopped because the sign looked so important. When he painted PLEASE KEEP OFF THE GRASS, they kept off because the sign was polite and sensible. When he painted GOOD FOOD, they just naturally became hungry.

People thanked the signmaker and paid him well. But the kind old man never failed to say, "I couldn't have done it without Norman's help."

Norman was the signmaker's assistant. Each day after school he cut wood, mixed colors, and painted simple signs.

"Soon I will have a shop of my own," said Norman.

"Perhaps," answered the signmaker, "but not before you clean these brushes."

One day after his work was done, Norman stood at a window over the sign shop and watched people. They stopped at the STOP sign. They entered at the ENTER sign. They ate under the GOOD FOOD sign.

"They do whatever the signs say!" said Norman to himself. "I wonder . . ." He crept into the shop while the signmaker napped. With brush and board he painted a sign of his own.

Early the next morning he put up the sign, then ran
back to his window to watch.

"No school?" muttered the principal. "How could I
forget such a thing?"

"No one informed me," said the teacher.

"Hooray!" cheered the children, and everyone went home.

"This is great!" cried Norman. He looked around town for another idea. "Oh," he said at last, "there is something I have always wanted to do."

**ANALYZE THE TEXT**

**Point of View** How does the principal feel about school being closed? How do the children feel?

The following day Norman jumped from the top of the fountain in the park. As he swam, he thought to himself, I can do lots of things with signs. Ideas filled his head.

That afternoon when Norman went to work, the signmaker said, "I must drive to the next town and paint a large sign on a storefront. I'll return tomorrow evening, so please lock up the shop tonight."

As soon as the signmaker was gone, Norman started making signs. He painted for hours and hours and hours.

In the morning people discovered new signs all around town.

Norman watched it all and laughed until tears came
to his eyes.  But soon he saw people becoming angry.

"The signmaker is playing tricks," they shouted.
"He has made fools of us!"

The teacher tore down the NO SCHOOL
TODAY sign.  Suddenly people were tearing down
all the signs—not just the new ones but every sign the
signmaker had ever painted.

Then the real trouble started. Without store signs, shoppers became confused. Without stop signs, drivers didn't know when to stop. Without street signs, firemen became lost.

In the evening when the signmaker returned from his work in the next town, he knew nothing of Norman's tricks. An angry crowd of people met him at the back door of his shop and chased him into the woods.

As Norman watched, he suddenly realized that without signs and without the signmaker, the town was in danger.

"It's all my fault!" cried Norman, but no one was listening.

Late that night the signmaker returned and saw a
light on in his shop.  Norman was feverishly painting.

While the town slept and the signmaker watched, Norman put up stop signs, shop signs, street signs, danger signs, and welcome signs; in and out signs, large and small signs, new and beautiful signs. He returned all his presents and cleared away the garbage at the grocery store. It was morning when he finished putting up his last sign for the entire town to see.

Then Norman packed his things and locked up
the shop. But as he turned to go, he discovered the
signmaker and all the townspeople gathered at the door.

"I know you're angry with me for what I did," said Norman with downcast eyes, "so I'm leaving."

"Oh, we were angry all right!" answered the school principal. "But we were also fools for obeying such signs without thinking."

"You told us you are sorry," said the signmaker, "and you fixed your mistakes. So stay, and work hard. One day this shop may be yours."

"Perhaps," answered Norman, hugging the old man, "but not before I finish cleaning those brushes."

# Dig Deeper

## Use Clues to Analyze the Text

Use these pages to learn about Text and Graphic Features and Point of View. Then read *The Signmaker's Assistant* again. Use what you learn to understand it better.

## Text and Graphic Features

In *The Signmaker's Assistant,* you read about a boy who changed all of the signs in his town. The pictures, or **graphic features,** in this story help you understand what is happening. You have to read the signs in the pictures to understand the problem.

When you read, use a chart like the one below to list the graphic features in the story and what they tell you about the characters, setting, or plot.

| Text or Graphic Feature | Page Number | Purpose |
|---|---|---|
| | | |

# Point of View

Characters in a story sometimes think about the same event in different ways. Each character has a different **point of view.** Look at page 140 again. Think about how the characters feel when Norman changes the signs. Norman thinks it is funny, but the townspeople are angry. As you read a character's words, think about how he or she might feel about what is happening.

# Your Turn

**Turn and Talk**

**How are signs helpful?** Think about the signs in *The Signmaker's Assistant.* Then think about signs that you have seen in your town. Discuss your ideas with a partner. Add your own ideas to what he or she says.

## Classroom Conversation

Now talk about these questions with the class.

1. How do the words and illustrations work together to help you understand this story?

2. Why do you think Norman is sorry for tricking the town? Explain your answer using text evidence.

3. What lesson does Norman learn?

### WRITE ABOUT READING ··············  my WriteSmart

**Response** Think about how the signmaker and Norman treat each other. Work with a partner. Write a short play about Norman and the signmaker. Show how they act toward each other during one part of the story. Take turns acting out each character's lines. Use a different voice for each character to show how each is feeling.

### Writing Tip

When you write a play, write each character's name followed by what he or she says.

# PLAY

ELA RL.2.6, RL.2.10

## GENRE

A **play** is a story people act out.

## TEXT FOCUS

**Dialogue** is the talk between two or more people in a play. Dialogue helps the reader get to know each character's point of view through his or her own words.

# The Trouble with Signs

## by Bebe Jaffe

### Cast of Characters
Ana

Ben

**Ben:** (steering a car) I'm glad we agreed to drive to the town meeting. We can look at the scenery.

**Ana:** (reading the pretend sign) Fresh berries. Turn left at the fork. Yum!

**Ben:** Where's the fork?

**Ana:** Do we need a fork to eat the berries?

**Ben:** I'm talking about a fork in the road!

**Ana:** I get it! You've got SO much wisdom, Ben.

**Ben:** I hope you are being polite and not teasing me.

**Ana:** (reading another sign) Do you have car trouble? Come to Polly's Place for some R and R. What's R and R?

**Ben:** R and R stands for Rest and Relaxation.

**Ana:** I'm glad that's cleared up, but do cars go to a special place for R and R?

**Ben:** (shaking his head) No, Ana. PEOPLE do.

**Ana:** Right! Listen to this sign! Have you failed in the kitchen? Are you tearing out your hair? Come to Carla's Cooking Class. Ouch! Do people tear their hair out because they overcooked a roast?

**Ben:** (losing patience) NO, Ana! That's just a saying. It means someone is getting frustrated.

**Ana:** Pull in! This is our meeting place.

**Ben:** Just in time! I'm tired of being your assistant.

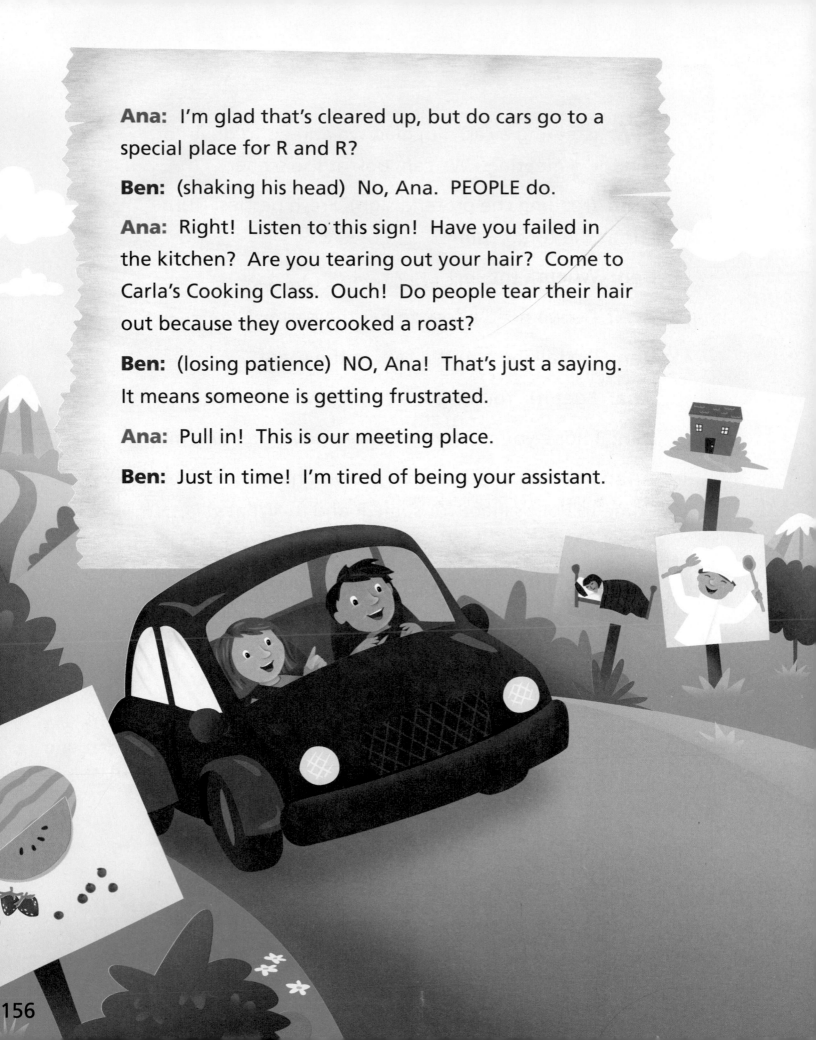

# Compare Texts

**Talk About Signs** Think about the signs that Norman makes and the signs in *The Trouble with Signs*. How do the signs in each story make the characters confused? Talk about it with a partner.

## TEXT TO SELF

**Make a Sign** Which sign from *The Signmaker's Assistant* do you think is the silliest? Make a silly sign for your classroom using words and pictures. Put it up for your class to see.

Make sure to laugh every 5 minutes!

## TEXT TO WORLD

**Connect to Social Studies** Look through *The Signmaker's Assistant* for signs that are helpful to people. Make a list with a partner. Talk about why the signs are important.

ELA RL.2.1, RL.2.7

# Grammar

**Commas in Dates and Places**  Every day has a **date.** A date tells the month, the number of the day, and the year.  Use a **comma** (,) between the number of the day and the year.  Also use a comma between the name of a city or town and the name of a state.

| Dates | Place Names |
|-------|-------------|
| May 2, 2017 | Austin, Texas |
| July 15, 2019 | Westville, Idaho |

 **Write the underlined date or place correctly.**

❶ The signmaker opened his shop on <u>June 4 1975</u>.

❷ The shop was in <u>Columbus Ohio</u>.

❸ The boy started work on <u>May 25 2018</u>.

❹ He came from <u>Logan Utah</u>.

Edit your writing carefully. Make sure you have used commas correctly when you write dates and names of places.

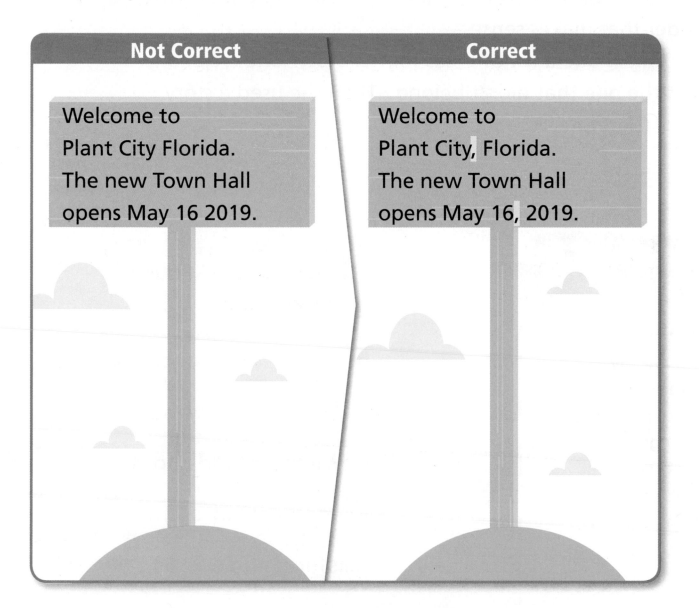

| Not Correct | Correct |
| --- | --- |
| Welcome to Plant City Florida. The new Town Hall opens May 16 2019. | Welcome to Plant City, Florida. The new Town Hall opens May 16, 2019. |

## Connect Grammar to Writing

**When you edit your story next week, be sure you have used commas, capital letters, and end marks correctly.**

# Narrative Writing

☑ **Organization** A **story** has a beginning, a middle, and an end. The events in a story should be told in an order that makes sense.

Julie made a list of ideas for her story. She crossed out the one that didn't belong. Then she used a story map to put her ideas in order.

## Writing Process Checklist

▶ **Prewrite**

☑ **Who are my characters?**

☑ **What happens at the beginning of the story?**

☑ **What happens in the middle?**

☑ **What happens at the end?**

**Draft**

**Revise**

**Edit**

**Publish and Share**

## Exploring a Topic

Girl has a pet.

~~She is a really good speller.~~

Pet has special powers.

They meet a sad giant.

Kids are afraid of the giant.

Hamster's name is Sparky.

Sparky knows when things are wrong.

# Beginning

Layla and Sparky go to the park.

They see a sign that the park is closed.

# Middle

They find a crying giant.

The giant tells them why he is crying.

Kids are scared of him.

# End

The kids see how gentle the giant is with Sparky.

The kids and the giant play together.

## Reading as a Writer

What differences do you see between Julie's list and her story map? How will putting your ideas in a story map help you plan your story?

I put my ideas in an order that would make sense in my story.

## 🔍 LANGUAGE DETECTIVE

**Talk About Words**
**Verbs** are words that name actions. Work with a partner. Find the Vocabulary words that are verbs. What are your clues? Use the verbs in new sentences.

# Vocabulary in Context

▶ Read each **Context Card**.

▶ Tell a story about two pictures. Use the Vocabulary words.

### 1 depended

The dog depended on its owner for food and water.

### 2 sore

The dog hurt its paw. The paw is sore.

### 3 sprang

The cat saw the food. She sprang toward her dish.

### 4 studied

Before getting a puppy, the girl studied a book about dog care.

### 5 gazing

This dog is gazing, or looking closely, at a squirrel.

### 6 hero

This dog is a hero. It saved the boy from getting hurt.

### 7 exercise

A dog needs exercise every day. This dog wants to run fast.

### 8 overlooked

They overlooked, or didn't see, where the dog was hiding.

# Read and Comprehend

## ☑ TARGET SKILL

**Compare and Contrast** In a story, the main characters will often go through some changes from the beginning to the end of a story. They grow and change because of the things that happen to them.

As you read *Dex: The Heart of a Hero*, you can compare and contrast to tell how Dex changes. You can use a diagram like the one below to **compare** things that are the same and **contrast** things that are different. Use the words and pictures in the story as text evidence for your ideas.

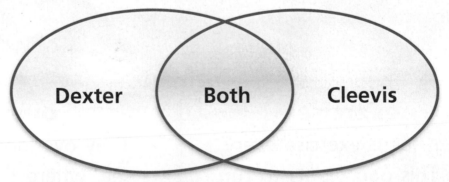

Dexter    Both    Cleevis

## ☑ TARGET STRATEGY

**Monitor/Clarify** If you don't understand why something is happening, stop and think. Find text evidence to figure out what doesn't make sense.

**ELA** RL.2.3, RL.2.4, RL.2.7, SL.2.1a

### What Heroes Do

A hero is someone who has done something brave or good to help others. You may know of some famous heroes from history. For example, Martin Luther King, Jr. was a hero who helped change unfair laws. Not all heroes are famous. Most people feel that firefighters and police officers are heroes. The person who takes care of you or who teaches you might be a hero.

You will read about a dog that wants to be a hero in *Dex: The Heart of a Hero.*

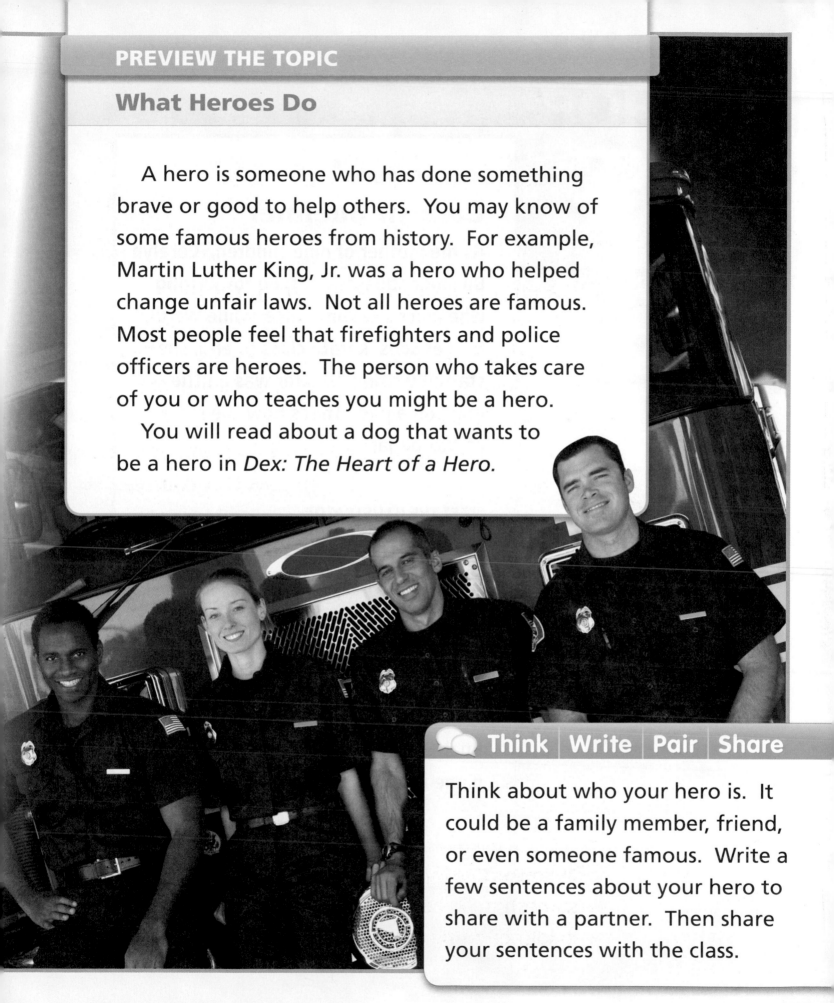

**Think | Write | Pair | Share**

Think about who your hero is. It could be a family member, friend, or even someone famous. Write a few sentences about your hero to share with a partner. Then share your sentences with the class.

# ANCHOR TEXT

## ✓ GENRE

A **fantasy** is a story that could not happen in real life. As you read, look for:

▸ events that could not really happen

▸ characters that are not found in real life

**MEET THE AUTHOR**

## Caralyn Buehner

As the mother of nine children, Caralyn Buehner squeezes in time for writing whenever she can. Once, while waiting for her sons' karate class to end, she started writing "Dexter was a little dog" on a pad. That's how the story of *Dex* began.

**MEET THE ILLUSTRATOR**

## Mark Buehner

As you read *Dex*, look carefully at the pictures. Mark Buehner likes to hide bunnies, dinosaurs, cats, and mice in his drawings. In case you're wondering, Mr. Buehner is Caralyn Buehner's husband, and their last name is pronounced *Bee-ner*.

# DEX
## The Heart of a Hero

by Caralyn Buehner
illustrated by Mark Buehner

**ESSENTIAL QUESTION**

What makes someone
a hero?

**D**exter was a little dog. His legs were little, his tail was little, his body was little. He looked like a plump sausage sitting on four little meatballs.

Being the size that he was, Dex was often overlooked. The other dogs grew tired of waiting for Dex to catch up when they played chase, and after a while they forgot to invite him at all. No one really seemed to notice him, except when Cleevis, the tomcat, demonstrated how he could stand right over Dex and not even ruffle his fur.

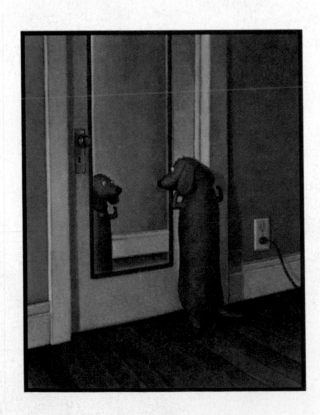

Yes, everything about Dex was little—except for his dreams. He wanted to be a HERO. He could just *see* it.

THE MIGHTY DEX FLEW UP INTO THE DARK AND STARRY NIGHT. . . .

But *wanting* and *being* are two different things. Dex lived on dreams until one day, after crawling out from under Cleevis yet again, he decided there had to be more to life than gazing at the underside of a cat. There had to be more to *him*. If he *could* be a hero, he *would*!

So Dex started training. He read every superhero comic book he could find. He watched every hero movie ever made. He went to the library.

FURIOUSLY HE STUDIED, KNOWING EVERYTHING DEPENDED ON HIM....

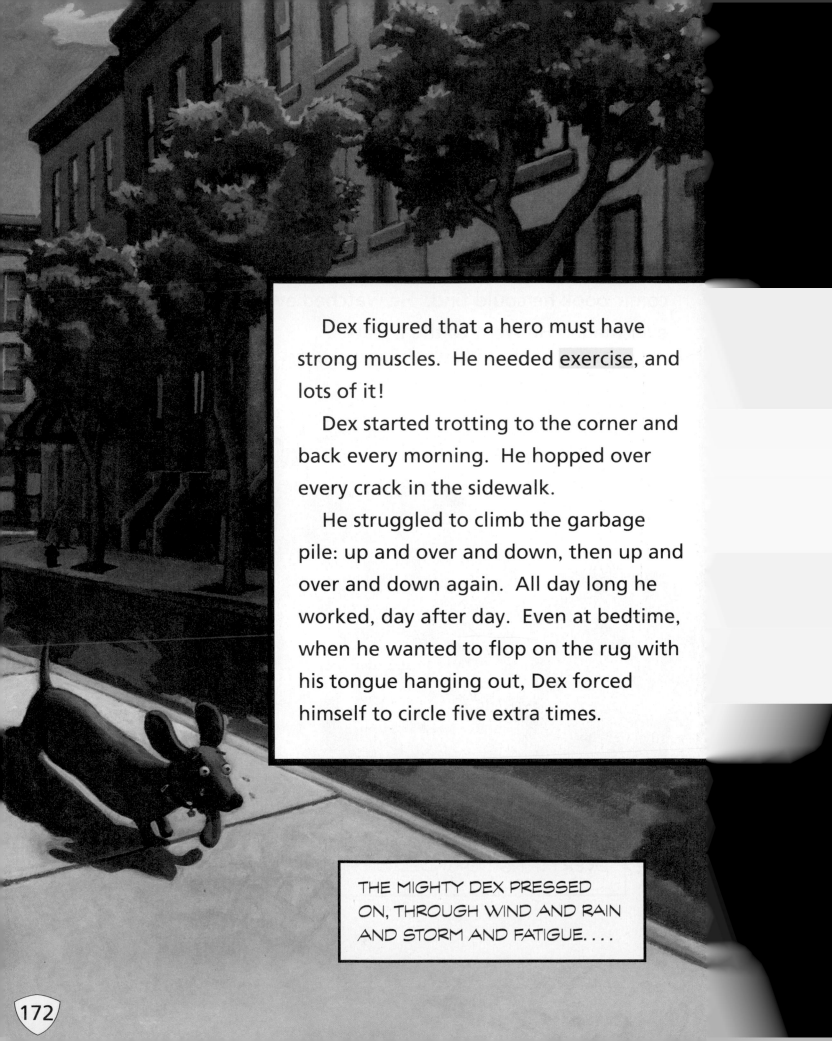

Dex figured that a hero must have strong muscles. He needed exercise, and lots of it!

Dex started trotting to the corner and back every morning. He hopped over every crack in the sidewalk.

He struggled to climb the garbage pile: up and over and down, then up and over and down again. All day long he worked, day after day. Even at bedtime, when he wanted to flop on the rug with his tongue hanging out, Dex forced himself to circle five extra times.

THE MIGHTY DEX PRESSED ON, THROUGH WIND AND RAIN AND STORM AND FATIGUE. . . .

When it got easier to run to the corner and back, Dex did it again, and then again. Then he dragged a sock filled with sand as he ran, and then *two* socks. When Cleevis was bored and stood in the middle of the sidewalk to block his way, Dex dropped to the ground and slid right under him. He was too busy to be bothered by Cleevis.

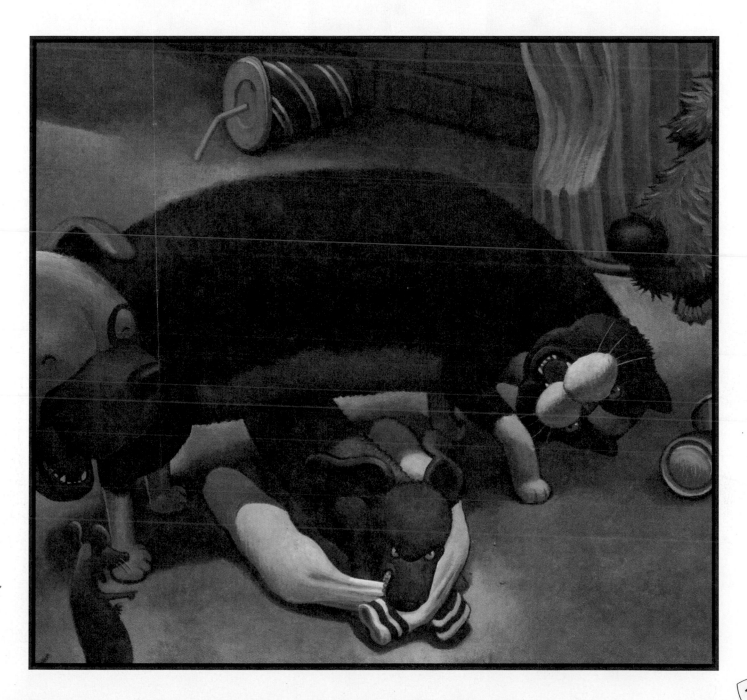

Dex was tired; he was sore. He was working
so hard that he almost forgot what he was
working for. But one night, as he dragged
himself to bed after his last set of push-ups, Dex
stopped in front of the mirror and flexed. He
could feel them! He could see them! Muscles!

FASTER THAN A ROLLING BALL, STRONGER THAN THE
TOUGHEST RAWHIDE, ABLE TO LEAP TALL FENCES IN A
SINGLE BOUND!

Now Dex didn't "take" the stairs—he skimmed
them! He leaped over hydrants; he vaulted up
curbs. He could jump over the garbage mountain
without touching the top! He could run like the
wind; he felt as if his legs had springs!

Only one thing was missing.

Finally, a small brown package arrived. Dex ripped it open.

His HERO suit! It was red, with a shiny green cape, and it fit like a glove. Dex loved the way it felt, he loved the way it looked, and he loved the feeling he had when he put it on.

He was ready.

## ANALYZE THE TEXT

**Figurative Language** What does the author mean when she says that Dex's hero suit "fit like a glove"?

WITH THE COURAGE OF A LION, THE STRENGTH OF A BEAR, AND THE HEART OF A HERO . . .

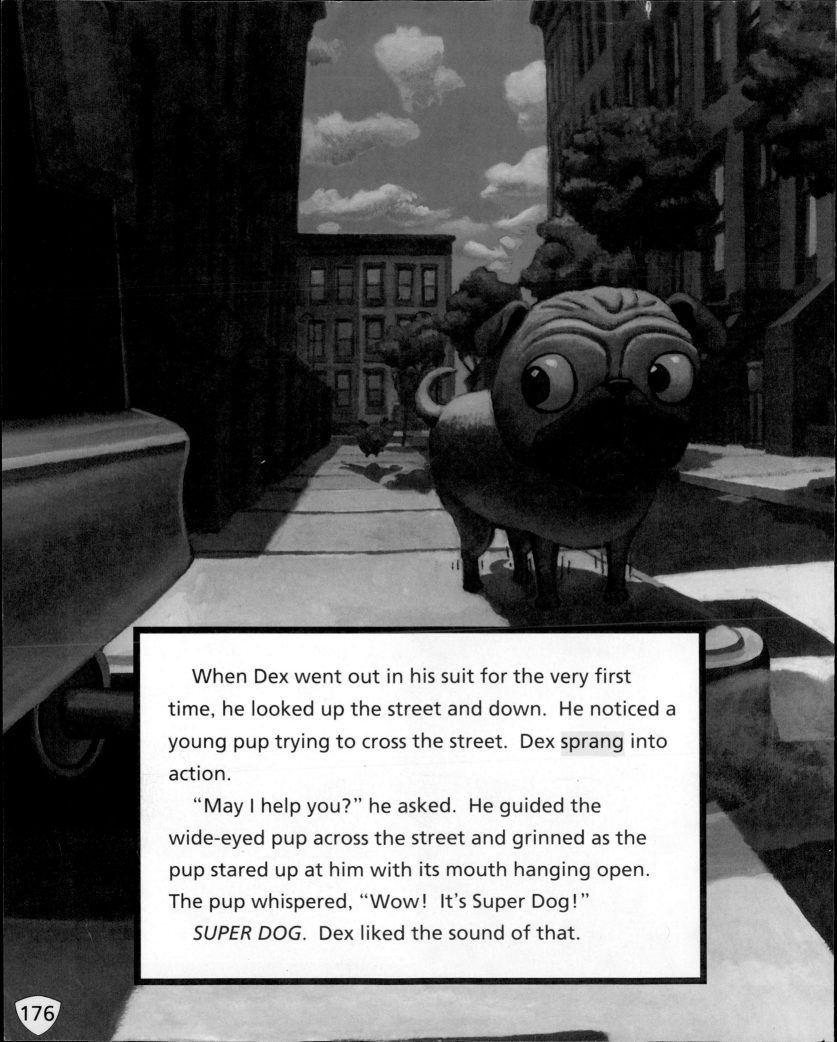

When Dex went out in his suit for the very first time, he looked up the street and down. He noticed a young pup trying to cross the street. Dex sprang into action.

"May I help you?" he asked. He guided the wide-eyed pup across the street and grinned as the pup stared up at him with its mouth hanging open. The pup whispered, "Wow! It's Super Dog!"

*SUPER DOG.* Dex liked the sound of that.

Of course, when Cleevis saw Dex, he just had to comment.

"Hey Dex, where's the party?"

Dex was so busy that he was able to ignore Cleevis—for the most part. The only time his face ever got red was when Cleevis yelled, "Where'd you get that dress-up?" Dex had to wonder if Cleevis saw anything but the suit. Didn't he understand that the suit was just a way to let people know he was there to help?

THE SUN GLINTED OFF OF HIS EMERALD CAPE AS SUPER DOG RACED TO THE RESCUE. . . .

There was a mouse he
saved from a sewer,

a purse snatcher he tackled;

he fixed his neighbor's
sprinkler;

he found a lost kitten, pulled a rat away from a live wire,

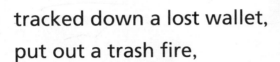

tracked down a lost wallet, put out a trash fire,

and organized a neighborhood cleanup day.

It seemed that now, whenever anyone needed help, they turned to Dex, and Dex had never been happier.

Late one evening there was a banging at the door. When Dex answered, it seemed as if the whole neighborhood was yipping and yeowling in a panic.

"It's Cleevis!" they shouted. "He's stuck in a tree. Hurry, Dex, hurry!"

Dex raised his eyebrows. It was not like Cleevis to move enough to get into any trouble.

In a flash he was dressed and ready.

IT WAS CLEARLY A DESPERATE SITUATION. . . .

As he got closer, Dex could see Cleevis. He had been chasing a squirrel to the top of the tree, but had slipped and was hanging by one claw from a slender branch.

He was yeowling for all he was worth.

"I'm slipping!" Cleevis screeched. "Help me!"

Dex looked desperately around for something to climb on. There were no boxes or ladders, not even any trash cans. Then Dex looked at the crowd.

OH, NO!

"Quick, everybody!" Dex shouted. "I've got an idea!" Dex leaped onto the end of the teeter-totter facing the tree, pushing it to the ground.

"Everybody on the other end! One! Two! Three!!!!"

All the animals jumped together on the other end of the teeter-totter, catapulting Dex into the air. He soared over the crowd, his ears and cape streaming out behind him. . . .

THE MIGHTY DEX FLEW UP INTO
THE DARK AND STARRY NIGHT....

185

Dex scrambled onto the branch next to
Cleevis.  Quickly he pulled off his cape and tied
its four corners onto the screeching cat.
"Jump!" Dex shouted.  "Jump, Cleevis!"

With an ear-piercing shriek, Cleevis let go. The billowing cape caught the air and parachuted the big cat to the ground. Dex backed up and slid to the ground amidst the cheers of the crowd.

Dex was bruised and tired, but he forgot his discomfort as Cleevis sheepishly lumbered over, still tangled in the green cape.

"Thanks, Dex. You really are a hero!"

Dex didn't think he could feel any better, but he did—just a little—the next day, when Cleevis sidled up next to him and whispered, "Say, Dex, could I be your partner?"

Dex looked the big tomcat up and down. It would take a *lot* of work to turn Cleevis into a hero. He could hardly wait.

"Sure," said Dex with a grin. "Sure."

**ANALYZE THE TEXT**

**Compare and Contrast** How has Cleevis changed by the end of the story?

# Dig Deeper

## Use Clues to Analyze the Text

Use these pages to learn about Comparing and Contrasting and Figurative Language. Then read *Dex: The Heart of a Hero* again. Use what you learn to understand it better.

## Compare and Contrast

In *Dex: The Heart of a Hero*, some of the characters change during the story. You can **compare** the characters' thoughts and feelings at the beginning and the end of the story by telling how they are the same. You can **contrast** by telling how they are different.

Words and pictures from the story are clues about how the characters change. Use a diagram like this for the beginning of the story and another for the end. Show how the characters changed.

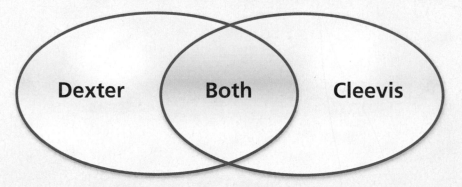

Dexter     Both     Cleevis

# Figurative Language

Authors sometimes tell how two things are the same using the word *like* or *as*. This is called a **simile.** A simile helps readers picture story details in their mind. For example, *The dog ran as fast as lightning* is a simile. The dog can't really run as fast as lightning, but the simile helps the reader understand that the dog is running fast. Look for examples of similes as you reread *Dex: The Heart of a Hero*.

# Your Turn

 **What makes someone a hero?** Discuss with a partner. Find text evidence from *Dex: The Heart of a Hero* to support your ideas. Speak one at a time. Add your own ideas to what your partner says.

## Classroom Conversation

Now talk about these questions with the class.

1 How does Dex and Cleevis's friendship change from the beginning to the end of the story?

2 Why is Dex happy that Cleevis wants to be his partner at the end of the story?

3 Think of other superhero stories you know. How is Dex like the superheroes in those stories?

### WRITE ABOUT READING

**Response** Think about how Dex helped Cleevis. Would you have helped someone who had been mean to you in the past? Write a paragraph to share your opinion.

### Writing Tip

Use linking words, such as *so* or *because,* to connect reasons with your ideas.

## INFORMATIONAL TEXT

# HEROES THEN AND NOW

What makes a hero?  A hero does something brave or works hard to help others.  A hero doesn't give up when things are hard.

Heroes come from different backgrounds and different places. They can be young or old.  All heroes are important people, whether they lived in the past or do good deeds today.

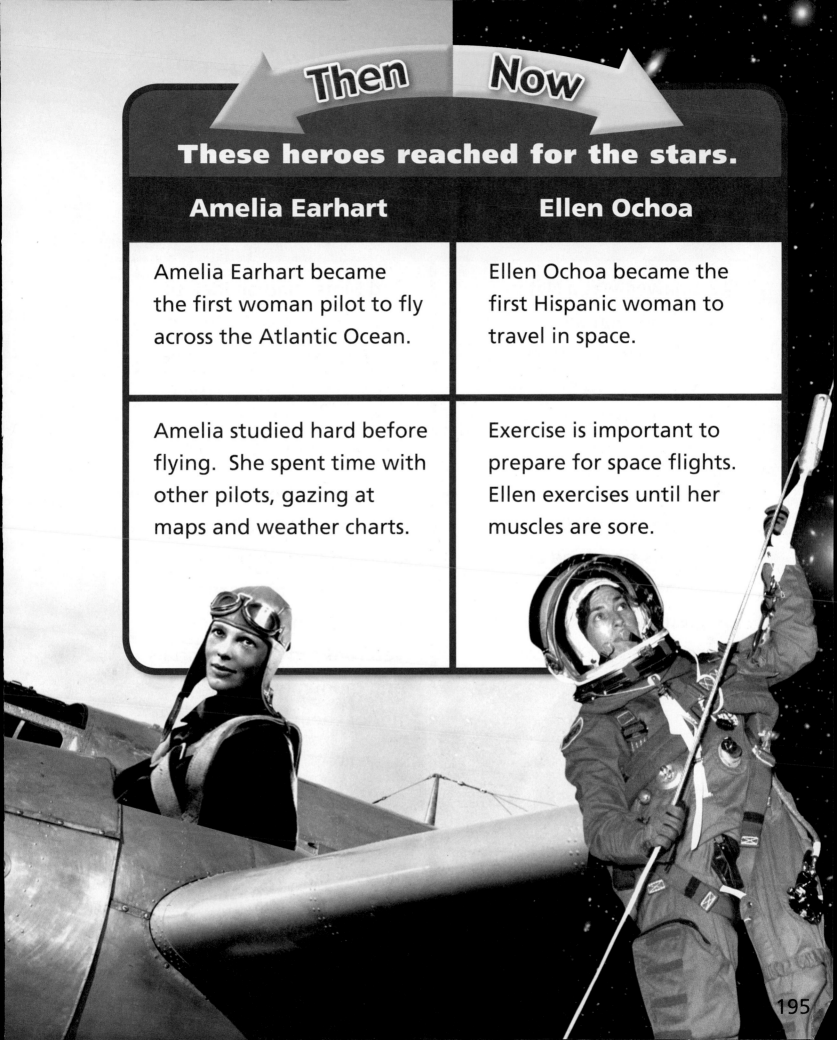

## Then ← → Now

### These heroes reached for the stars.

| Amelia Earhart | Ellen Ochoa |
|---|---|
| Amelia Earhart became the first woman pilot to fly across the Atlantic Ocean. | Ellen Ochoa became the first Hispanic woman to travel in space. |
| Amelia studied hard before flying. She spent time with other pilots, gazing at maps and weather charts. | Exercise is important to prepare for space flights. Ellen exercises until her muscles are sore. |

## Then ⟷ Now

## The heroes in this chart helped others.

| Sacagawea | Earl Morse |
|---|---|
| Sacagawea was a Native American woman who lived over 200 years ago. She helped a group of early American explorers. | Earl Morse had an idea to honor veterans. Veterans are men and women who have been in the military. Some veterans were in the military during times of war. |
| Sacagawea helped the explorers find food and learn about the land. She helped them talk to Native Americans that they met. | Morse helped to start a group that helps pay for veterans to travel to Washington, D.C. There the veterans can see memorials and monuments that honor them. |

# Compare Texts

What Makes a Hero?

## TEXT TO TEXT

**Discuss Heroes** Think about Dex and the heroes in *Heroes Then and Now*. What makes them heroes? In a small group, make a poster to show your ideas. Include words and pictures. Present the poster to the class.

## TEXT TO SELF

**Share a Story** Think of a time when you felt the way Dex does at the beginning of *Dex: The Heart of a Hero*. What did you do? Tell a partner.

## TEXT TO WORLD

**Talk About Dog Heroes** What does Dex do to help the other animals? What are some ways dogs can help in your community? Share your ideas with the class.

ELA RL.2.1, RI.2.9, W.2.8

# Grammar

**Commas in a Series** When there are three or more **nouns** in a sentence, separate them with **commas** and the word *and*. Also use commas and the word *and* when there are three or more **verbs** in a sentence.

| Series of Nouns | Series of Verbs |
|---|---|
| The dogs, cats, and birds saw Dex. | He jumped, hopped, and climbed. |
| My sister, my brother, and I want to be heroes. | We stretch, flex, and train our muscles. |

**Try This!** **Read the sentences aloud with a partner. Tell where to add commas to make the sentences correct. Then write the sentences correctly.**

❶ The cat scratched howled and hissed.

❷ Dex helped boys girls and animals.

❸ He studied ran and practiced.

Short, choppy sentences can be combined. This will make your writing smoother.

## Short, Choppy Sentences

| The dog leaped over boxes. | The dog leaped over logs. | The dog leaped over fences. |

## Smoother Sentence with Commas

The dog leaped over boxes, logs, and fences.

## Connect Grammar to Writing

When you revise your story, try combining some short sentences.

# Narrative Writing

☑ **Organization** A good **story** starts with a strong beginning. If the beginning of your story is interesting, it makes your readers want to read more.

Julie wrote a draft of a story about a girl and her special pet. Later, she revised the story's beginning.

## Writing Process Checklist

**Prewrite**

**Draft**

▶ **Revise**

☑ Does my story have a beginning, middle, and end?

☑ Does the beginning make the reader want to read more?

☑ Did I include interesting details?

☑ Did I tell how the problem is solved?

**Edit**

**Publish and Share**

### Revised Draft

Layla had a pet hamster named Sparky. Sparky was not like any other hamster. He could do something no other ∧ hamster could do.

Sparky was small and brown. Layla thought he was amazing. ∧ He knew when things were wrong.

# Sparky and the Giant
by Julie Martine

Layla had a pet hamster named Sparky. Sparky was not like any other hamster. He could do something no other hamster could do.

Sparky was small and brown. Layla thought he was amazing. He knew when things were wrong.

One day Layla and Sparky were walking in the park. Sparky started making noise and running around in Layla's pocket.

"What's up, Sparky?" Layla said as she gently patted her pocket.

## Reading as a Writer

How does Julie make her beginning more interesting? How can your beginning be more interesting?

I made the beginning more interesting.

# Write a Story

**TASK**  Look back at *My Name Is Gabriela* and *Heroes Then and Now*.  Gabriela Mistral and Amelia Earhart took adventures around the same time in history.  Imagine you lived at that time and went on an adventure together.  Write a story telling about your adventure to share with your classmates.  Use information from both texts to help you.

**PLAN**

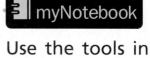

Use the tools in your eBook to remember details about Gabriela Mistral and Amelia Earhart.

**Gather Information**  Talk with a partner about *My Name Is Gabriela* and *Heroes Then and Now*. What things about each woman can you put into your story?

Then write ideas for your story in a story map.

- Who are the other characters in your story?

- What adventure will you take and where?

- What is the problem?

- How will your story end?

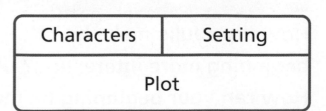

| Characters | Setting |
|------------|---------|
| Plot ||

Write your draft in *my*WriteSmart.

**Write Your Story** Use the information below to help you organize your story.

## Beginning

Write an interesting beginning. Use your story map for ideas. Describe how you meet Gabriela and Amelia, and introduce the problem. Use pronouns correctly.

## Middle

Tell about the important events in order. Leave out any events that don't help tell the story.

## Ending

Give the story a strong ending. The ending should answer these questions for the reader:

- How do the characters solve the problem?
- How do the characters feel when the story ends?

## REVISE

**Review Your Draft** Read your writing and make it better. Use the Checklist.

Have a partner read your draft. Talk about how you can make it better.

 Does my story have a beginning that will get the reader's attention?

 Did I include details from the texts to show what Gabriela and Amelia are like?

 Do the characters face a problem and solve it?

 Did I use pronouns correctly?

## PRESENT

**Share** Write or type a copy of your story. Add pictures. Pick a way to share.

- Read your story to classmates.
- Ask classmates to help you act out your story.

# UNIT 5

# Changes, Changes Everywhere

**Stream to Start**

> ❝ The need for change bulldozed a road down the center of my mind. ❞
>
> — Maya Angelou

## Performance Task Preview

At the end of this unit, you will think about two of the stories you have read. Then you will use examples from each story to write about what it means to be a good friend.

hmhfyi.com

**Channel One News®**

Penguin Chick

by Betty Tatham · illustrated by Helen K. Davie

Emperor Penguins

## 🔍 LANGUAGE DETECTIVE

**Talk About Words**
Work with a partner. Take turns asking and answering questions about the photos. Use the Vocabulary words in your questions and answers.

🗐 myNotebook

Add new words to **myWordList**. Use them in your speaking and writing.

# Vocabulary in Context

▶ **Read each Context Card.**

▶ **Place the Vocabulary words in alphabetical order.**

**1 webbed**
A penguin is a bird with big, webbed feet. Its toes are joined by thin skin.

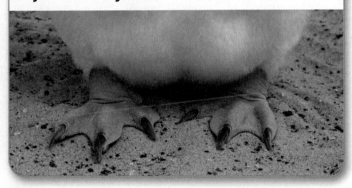

**2 waterproof**
Penguins' feathers are waterproof, which keeps the birds warm and dry.

### 3 steer

Webbed feet help penguins steer through the cold Antarctic water.

### 4 whistle

It is very cold in Antarctica. The wind makes a high, sharp sound, like a whistle.

### 5 otherwise

The penguin father keeps his egg warm. Otherwise, the egg might get too cold.

### 6 junior

At five months, a junior penguin is still younger than an adult.

### 7 slippery

The scientist tries not to slide on the ice. The ice is very slippery to walk on.

### 8 finally

These penguin chicks finally grew up and became adult penguins.

# Read and Comprehend

**Main Idea and Details** The **topic** is what a whole selection is about. The **main idea** tells more about the topic. **Details** give the reader more information about the main idea. You can use a chart to show the main idea and the details that tell more about it.

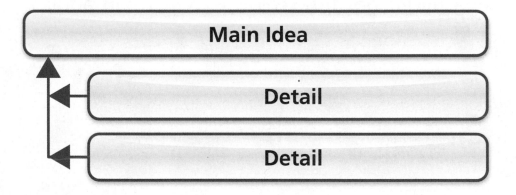

| Main Idea |
|---|
| Detail |
| Detail |

✓ **TARGET STRATEGY**

**Infer/Predict** Use clues, or text evidence, to figure out more about the information in the text.

## Animal Development

Animals change as they grow. Many baby animals stay with at least one parent while they are young. The parent helps the young animal stay safe and find food. As a young animal grows, it becomes more like an adult. Its appearance may change. It starts to look like an adult animal. It also learns to take care of itself. The young animal is then able to live on its own.

You will learn about how penguin parents care for a young penguin in *Penguin Chick*.

###  Talk About It

What do you know about penguins? What would you like to know about them? Talk about your ideas with the class.

- ▶ Listen carefully to others.
- ▶ Stay on topic.
- ▶ Ask questions to understand.

Penguin Chick

by Betty Tatham · illustrated by Helen K. Davie

☑ **GENRE**

**Narrative nonfiction** tells a true story about a topic. As you read, look for:

▸ a setting that is real
▸ events in time order
▸ facts and information

**MEET THE AUTHOR**

# Betty Tatham

"I only write about subjects I love, or those I want to learn more about," says Betty Tatham. Penguins are her favorite animal, so she wrote *Penguin Chick*. After seeing playful otters at the Monterey Bay Aquarium in California, she wrote *Baby Sea Otter*. A trip to China and the opportunity to hold a five-month-old panda cub led Ms. Tatham to create a book about these rare animals.

# Penguin Chick

by Betty Tatham

**ESSENTIAL QUESTION**

How do animals care for their young?

212

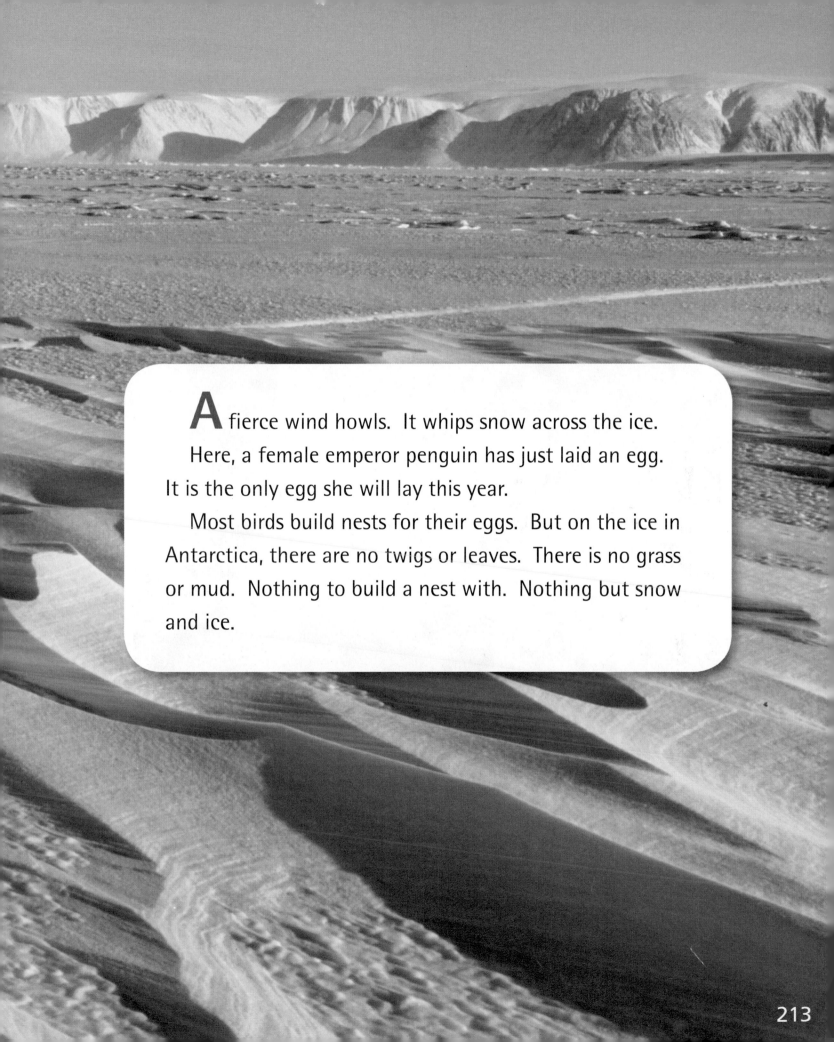

A fierce wind howls. It whips snow across the ice. Here, a female emperor penguin has just laid an egg. It is the only egg she will lay this year.

Most birds build nests for their eggs. But on the ice in Antarctica, there are no twigs or leaves. There is no grass or mud. Nothing to build a nest with. Nothing but snow and ice.

The new penguin father uses his beak to scoop the egg onto his webbed feet.

He tucks it under his feather-covered skin, into a special place called a brood patch. The egg will be as snug and warm there as if it were in a sleeping bag.

One of the penguin parents must stay with the egg to keep it warm. But where penguins lay their eggs, there is no food for them to eat.

The penguin father is bigger and fatter than the mother. He can live longer without food. So the father penguin stays with the egg while the mother travels to the sea to find food.

The two parents sing together before the mother penguin leaves.

**ANALYZE THE TEXT**

**Cause and Effect** Why does the mother penguin have to leave?

Along with many other penguins, the mother penguin leaves the rookery, where she laid her egg.

The mother walks or slides on her belly. This is called tobogganing. She uses her flippers and webbed feet to push herself forward over ice and snow.

Because it's winter in Antarctica, water near the shore is frozen for many miles. After three days the mother penguin comes to the end of the ice. She dives into the water to hunt for fish, squid, and tiny shrimplike creatures called krill.

Back at the rookery, the penguin fathers form a group called a huddle. They stand close together for warmth. Each one keeps his own egg warm.

For two months the penguin father always keeps his egg on his feet. When he walks, he shuffles his feet so the egg doesn't roll away. He sleeps standing up. He has no food to eat, but the fat on his body keeps him alive.

**ANALYZE THE TEXT**

**Main Idea and Details** What is the main idea on this page? Which details support the main idea?

Finally he feels the chick move inside the egg. The chick pecks and pecks and pecks. In about three days the egg cracks open.

The chick is wet. But soon his soft feathers, called down, dry and become fluffy and gray. The father still keeps the chick warm in the brood patch. Sometimes the chick pokes his head out. But while he's so little, he must stay covered. And he must stay on his father's feet. Otherwise the cold would kill him.

The father talks to the chick in his trumpet voice. The chick answers with a whistle.

The father's trumpet call echoes across the ice. The penguin mother is on her way back to the rookery, but she can't hear him. She's still too far away. If the mother doesn't come back soon with food, the chick will die.

Two days pass before the mother can hear the father penguin's call.

At last the mother arrives at the rookery. She cuddles close to her chick and trumpets to him. He whistles back. With her beak she brushes his soft gray down.

The mother swallowed many fish before she left the ocean. She brings some of this food back up from her stomach and feeds her chick. She has enough food to keep him fed for weeks. He stays on her feet and snuggles into her brood patch.

The father is very hungry, so he travels to open water. There he dives to hunt for food. Weeks later the father returns with more food for the chick.

Each day the parents preen, or brush, the chick's downy coat with their beaks. This keeps the down fluffy and keeps the chick warm.

As the chick gets bigger, he and the other chicks no longer need to stay on their parents' feet. Instead they stay together to keep warm.

This group of chicks is called a crèche, or a nursery. The chick now spends most of his time here. But he still rushes to his mother or father to be fed when either one comes back from the ocean.

Sometimes the chick and the other young penguins dig their beaks into the ice to help them walk up a slippery hill. They toboggan down fast on their fluffy bellies.

The chick grows and grows. After five months, he has grown into a junior penguin. He is old enough to travel to the ocean.

Now he has a waterproof coat of feathers, instead of fluffy down. He can swim in the icy cold ocean because his feathers keep him dry and warm.

The young penguin spends most of his time in the water. He swims, flapping his flippers as if he were flying underwater. He uses his webbed feet to steer wherever he wants to go.

He catches a fish with his beak and swallows it headfirst.

Now the young penguin can catch his own food and take care of himself. In about five years he'll find a mate. Then he'll take care of his own egg until the chick can hatch.

# Dig Deeper

## Use Clues to Analyze the Text

Use these pages to learn about Main Idea and Details and Cause and Effect. Then read *Penguin Chick* again. Use what you learn to understand it better.

## Main Idea and Details

You read about how penguins grow in *Penguin Chick*. The **topic** is what a selection is all about. Each paragraph has a **main idea. Details** tell more about each main idea. Look at page 225. The main idea is that a young penguin spends most of its time in water. The other sentences tell details about what the penguin does in the water.

As you reread, use a chart like the one below to show each main idea and its details.

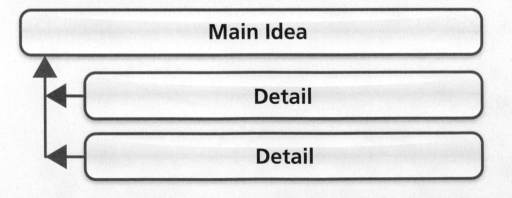

| Main Idea |
|-----------|
| Detail |
| Detail |

# Cause and Effect

One event often makes another event happen. For example, the father penguin keeps an egg warm between his feet. Months later, the egg hatches. The penguin keeping the egg warm is a **cause.** The egg hatching is the **effect.**

Thinking about cause and effect can help you understand how ideas are connected. As you read, ask yourself what happens and why.

# Your Turn

 **How do animals care for their young?** Look for paragraphs in *Penguin Chick* that focus on this topic. Use text evidence in those paragraphs to help you answer. Discuss your answer with a partner. Take turns listening and speaking.

## Classroom Conversation

Now talk about these questions with the class.

1. How do the parents work together to care for a penguin chick? Give examples using text evidence.

2. Why do you think the father penguin calls to the mother penguin when the chick has hatched?

3. How are penguins different from other birds?

### WRITE ABOUT READING ·····················

**Response** Imagine that you are selling land to penguins in Antarctica. With a small group, write an ad for the land you want to sell. Be sure to include in your ad all the things a penguin chick needs to survive.

## Writing Tip

Use commas and the word *and* to separate three or more nouns in a sentence.

# INFORMATIONAL TEXT

Emperor Penguins

# Emperor Penguins

Most penguins live in the southern part of the world below the equator. Some penguins live in cold areas, and some penguins live in the warmer areas near the equator.

One type of penguin that lives where it is cold is the emperor penguin.

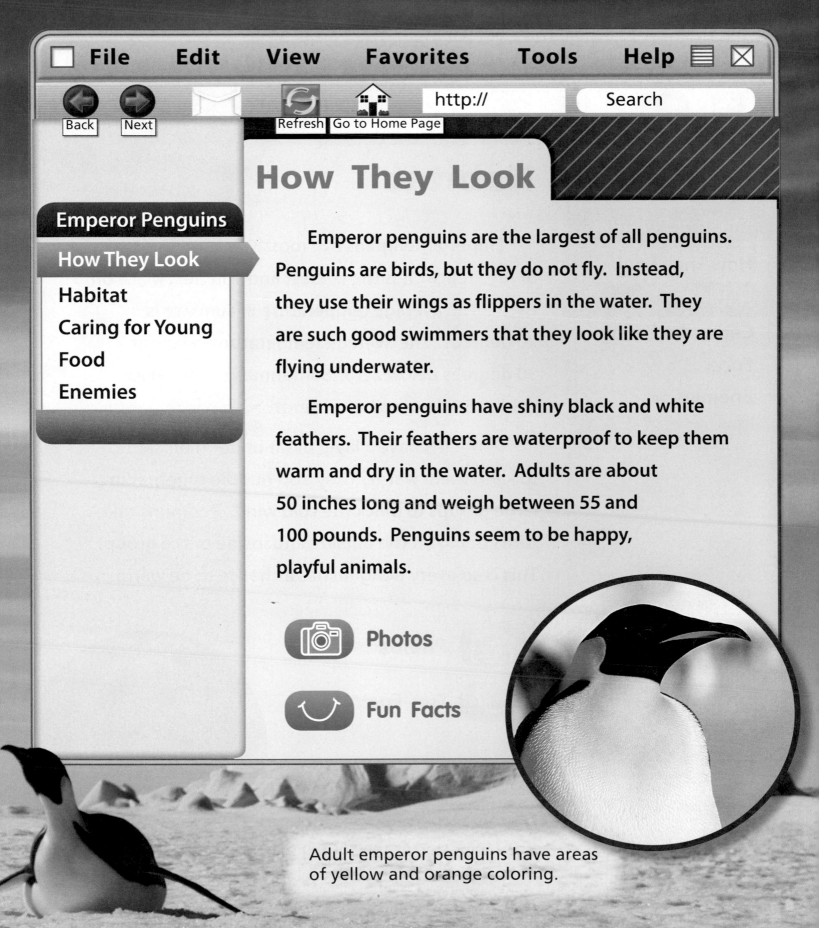

http://   Search

Back   Next   Refresh  Go to Home Page

# How They Look

**Emperor Penguins**

- **How They Look**
- Habitat
- Caring for Young
- Food
- Enemies

Emperor penguins are the largest of all penguins. Penguins are birds, but they do not fly. Instead, they use their wings as flippers in the water. They are such good swimmers that they look like they are flying underwater.

Emperor penguins have shiny black and white feathers. Their feathers are waterproof to keep them warm and dry in the water. Adults are about 50 inches long and weigh between 55 and 100 pounds. Penguins seem to be happy, playful animals.

Photos

Fun Facts

Adult emperor penguins have areas of yellow and orange coloring.

| File | Edit | View | Favorites | Tools | Help |
|------|------|------|-----------|-------|------|

Back    Next    Refresh   Go to Home Page    http://    Search

# Habitat

**Emperor Penguins**

How They Look

Habitat

Caring for Young

Food

Enemies

Emperor penguins live mostly around the coast of Antarctica. It is the coldest and windiest place on Earth. The average temperature in summer is 20 degrees. The average temperature in winter is 30 degrees below zero. Sometimes it can get as cold as 50 degrees below zero!

Penguins have a layer of fat under their skin to keep them warm. They also huddle together in large groups to block the cold wind. Penguins take turns being on the outside and inside of the group. This is so every penguin has a chance to be warm.

 Photos

 Fun Facts

Antarctica is located at the South Pole.

# Compare Texts

## TEXT TO TEXT

**Discuss Penguins** Think about what you learned in *Penguin Chick* and *Emperor Penguins*. What information is the same and different in the selections? Discuss your ideas with a small group.

## TEXT TO SELF

**Discuss Changing** How does a penguin chick grow and change? Tell a partner about two ways you have changed since you started second grade.

## TEXT TO WORLD

**Connect to Science** Work with a partner. Use reference books to find pictures and facts about a bird you both like. Write two facts about it. Share what you found with another pair of partners.

ELA RI.2.1, RI.2.9, W.2.7

# Grammar

**What Is an Adjective?** An **adjective** is a word that describes how something looks, tastes, or smells. An adjective can also describe how something sounds or how it feels to touch. Some examples of adjectives are shown in the chart below.

| Looks | Tastes or Smells | Sounds | Feels |
|-------|------------------|--------|-------|
| yellow | sweet | buzzing | crunchy |
| big | rotten | quiet | warm |
| pretty | spicy | loud | hard |

**Try This!** **Write the adjective in each sentence. Tell if the adjective describes how something looks, tastes, smells, sounds, or feels.**

❶ The penguin chick ate a tasty meal.

❷ The birds flop against the white snow.

❸ The egg sits on the penguin's webbed feet.

❹ We heard the noisy birds.

Sometimes you may write two sentences with adjectives that tell about the same noun. Join the sentences using the word *and* between the two adjectives. This will make your writing better.

### Short, Choppy Sentences

Penguin chicks are cute.

Penguin chicks are fuzzy.

### Longer, Smoother Sentence

Penguin chicks are cute and fuzzy.

## Connect Grammar to Writing

When you revise your problem-solution paragraph, try to combine sentences that have adjectives telling about the same noun.

# Informative Writing

**☑ Elaboration** When you write to inform, use exact words to give your reader more information.

   Matt drafted a **problem-solution paragraph** about how to solve a problem at his school.  Later, he revised by adding some exact words.

## Writing Checklist

**☑ Purpose**
Did I clearly state the solution to the problem?

**☑ Organization**
Did I start by telling what the problem is?

**☑ Elaboration**
Did I use exact words?

**☑ Conventions**
Did I use resources to help me spell all the words correctly?

## Revised Draft

   Our class has been studying

penguins.  Most of us have only
                                    Where could we see live penguins?
seen penguins on television.
                              ∧
The students in our class
   ~~Some people~~ voted on how to
∧
                          problem
solve this ~~thing~~.  We can go on
            ∧
                   to the aquarium
a field trip.
           ∧

# Live Penguins
by Matt Knightley

Our class has been studying penguins. Most of us have only seen penguins on television. Where could we see live penguins? The students in our class voted on how to solve this problem. We can go on a field trip to the aquarium. They have a penguin exhibit there. This way we can see live penguins close up.

## Reading as a Writer

**Which exact words did Matt add to give the reader more information? Which exact words can you add to your writing?**

I changed words and added words to give more information.

239

The Stories Julian Tells

Ann Cameron

How to Make a Kite

## 🔍 LANGUAGE DETECTIVE

**Talk About Words**
A verb's tense tells if something happened in the past, is happening now, or will happen in the future. Work with a partner. Find the Vocabulary words that are verbs. Then say the sentence again with the verb in a different tense.

# Vocabulary in Context

▶ Read each **Context Card.**

▶ Make up a new sentence that uses one of the Vocabulary words.

**1** **knot**
The boy showed how a strong knot in a rope can hold things together.

**2** **copy**
You can copy the outline of your hand by tracing over it onto a chalkboard.

### 3 planning

They are planning to fly their kite at the park today.

### 4 lonely

She misses her friend who moved to another town. She is lonely.

### 5 heavily

It was raining heavily. The umbrella kept them from getting soaking wet.

### 6 seriously

The boy takes playing chess seriously. He does not laugh or joke around.

### 7 answered

When the phone rang, she answered it and said hello.

### 8 guessed

The boy hid his eyes. He guessed that his friend was hiding behind a big tree.

The Stories Julian Tells

# Read and Comprehend

**Understanding Characters** Julian is the main character in *Gloria Who Might Be My Best Friend*. He talks, acts, and thinks like a real person. You can use clues in the words and pictures to figure out what the characters are like and why they act the way they do. List story clues, or text evidence, in a chart like this one.

| Character | What Happens | Words, Thoughts, Actions |
|---|---|---|
|  |  |  |

☑ **TARGET STRATEGY**

**Question** Ask questions about what you are reading. Look for text evidence to answer your questions.

## Following Directions

Directions tell you how to do things. Following directions helps you do things the right way. If you don't follow directions, you might have a problem. Think about what might happen if you didn't follow the directions for making cookies. The cookies probably wouldn't taste very good! When do you follow directions?

Julian and Gloria in *Gloria Who Might Be My Best Friend* follow directions to make a special kite together.

 **Think | Pair | Share**

Think about something simple to do, such as putting on a jacket. Give your partner directions for the task with at least three steps. Then follow the directions your partner has for you. Share what you learned with the class.

# ANCHOR TEXT

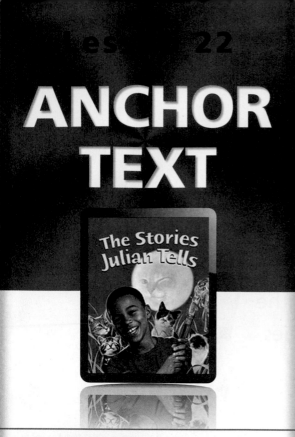

*The Stories Julian Tells*

## ✓ GENRE

**Realistic fiction** is a story that could happen in real life. As you read, look for:

- a setting that could be a real place
- characters who act like real people
- story events that could really happen

**MEET THE AUTHOR**

## ANN CAMERON

Sitting in a restaurant eating ice cream is Ann Cameron's favorite way to write. She has written many books about Julian and Gloria, including *Julian's Glorious Summer* and *Gloria's Way*.

**MEET THE ILLUSTRATOR**

## MIKE REED

Mike Reed makes his home in Minnesota. There he teaches college art classes for students who want to learn how to use a computer to create artwork.

# Gloria
## Who Might Be My Best Friend

### FROM THE STORIES JULIAN TELLS

by Ann Cameron        selection illustrated by Mike Reed

**ESSENTIAL QUESTION**

How do friends help
each other?

245

If you have a girl for a friend, people find out and tease you. That's why I didn't want a girl for a friend—not until this summer, when I met Gloria.

It happened one afternoon when I was walking down the street by myself. My mother was visiting a friend of hers, and Huey was visiting a friend of his. Huey's friend is five and so I think he is too young to play with. And there aren't any kids just my age. I was walking down the street feeling lonely.

A block from our house I saw a moving van in front of a brown house, and men were carrying in chairs and tables and bookcases and boxes full of I don't know what. I watched for a while, and suddenly I heard a voice right behind me.

"Who are you?"

I turned around and there was a girl in a yellow dress. She looked the same age as me. She had curly hair that was braided into two pigtails with red ribbons at the ends.

"I'm Julian," I said. "Who are you?"

"I'm Gloria," she said. "I come from Newport. Do you know where Newport is?"

I wasn't sure, but I didn't tell Gloria. "It's a town on the ocean," I said.

"Right," Gloria said. "Can you turn a cartwheel?"

She turned sideways herself and did two cartwheels on the grass.

I had never tried a cartwheel before, but I tried to copy Gloria. My hands went down in the grass, my feet went up in the air, and—I fell over.

I looked at Gloria to see if she was laughing at me. If she was laughing at me, I was going to go home and forget about her.

But she just looked at me very seriously and said, "It takes practice," and then I liked her.

**ANALYZE THE TEXT**

**Understanding Characters** What do you learn about Gloria from what she says and does after Julian does a cartwheel?

"I know where there's a bird's nest in your yard,"
I said.

"Really?" Gloria said. "There weren't any trees in
the yard, or any birds, where I lived before."

I showed her where a robin lives and has eggs.
Gloria stood up on a branch and looked in. The
eggs were small and pale blue. The mother robin
squawked at us, and she and the father robin flew
around our heads.

"They want us to go away," Gloria said. She got down from the branch, and we went around to the front of the house and watched the moving men carry two rugs and a mirror inside.

"Would you like to come over to my house?" I said.

"All right," Gloria said, "if it is all right with my mother." She ran in the house and asked.

It was all right, so Gloria and I went to my house, and I showed her my room and my games and my rock collection, and then I made strawberry punch and we sat at the kitchen table and drank it.

"You have a red mustache on your mouth," Gloria said.

"You have a red mustache on your mouth, too," I said.

Gloria giggled, and we licked off the mustaches with our tongues.

"I wish you'd live here a long time," I told Gloria.

Gloria said, "I wish I would too."

"I know the best way to make wishes," Gloria said.

"What's that?" I asked.

"First you make a kite. Do you know how to make one?"

"Yes," I said, "I know how." I know how to make good kites because my father taught me. We make them out of two crossed sticks and folded newspaper.

"All right," Gloria said, "that's the first part of making wishes that come true. So let's make a kite."

We went out into the garage and spread out sticks and newspaper and made a kite. I fastened on the kite string and went to the closet and got rags for the tail.

"Do you have some paper and two pencils?" Gloria asked. "Because now we make the wishes."

I didn't know what she was planning, but I went in the house and got pencils and paper.

"All right," Gloria said. "Every wish you want to have come true you write on a long thin piece of paper. You don't tell me your wishes, and I don't tell you mine. If you tell, your wishes don't come true. Also, if you look at the other person's wishes, your wishes don't come true."

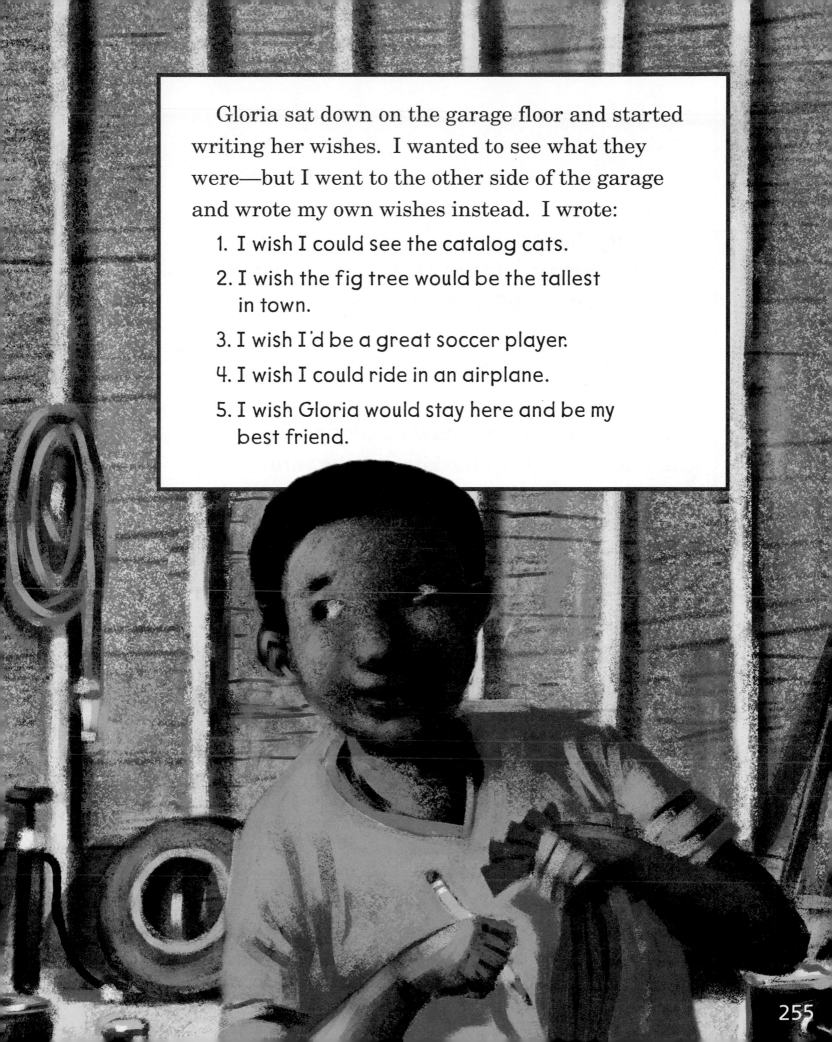

Gloria sat down on the garage floor and started writing her wishes. I wanted to see what they were—but I went to the other side of the garage and wrote my own wishes instead. I wrote:

1. I wish I could see the catalog cats.
2. I wish the fig tree would be the tallest in town.
3. I wish I'd be a great soccer player.
4. I wish I could ride in an airplane.
5. I wish Gloria would stay here and be my best friend.

I folded my five wishes in my fist and went over to Gloria.

"How many wishes did you make?" Gloria asked.

"Five," I said. "How many did you make?"

"Two," Gloria said.

I wondered what they were.

"Now we put the wishes on the tail of the kite," Gloria said. "Every time we tie one piece of rag on the tail, we fasten a wish in the knot. You can put yours in first."

I fastened mine in, and then Gloria fastened in hers, and we carried the kite into the yard.

"You hold the tail," I told Gloria, "and I'll pull."

We ran through the back yard with the kite, passed the garden and the fig tree, and went into the open field beyond our yard.

The kite started to rise. The tail jerked heavily like a long white snake. In a minute the kite passed the roof of my house and was climbing toward the sun.

**ANALYZE THE TEXT**

**Figurative Language** Why does the author describe the kite's tail as "like a long white snake"?

We stood in the open field, looking up at it. I was wishing I would get my wishes.

"I know it's going to work!" Gloria said.

"How do you know?"

"When we take the kite down," Gloria told me, "there shouldn't be one wish in the tail. When the wind takes all your wishes, that's when you know it's going to work."

The kite stayed up for a long time. We both held the string. The kite looked like a tiny black spot in the sun, and my neck got stiff from looking at it.

"Shall we pull it in?" I asked.

"All right," Gloria said.

We drew the string in more and more until, like a tired bird, the kite fell at our feet.

We looked at the tail. All our wishes were gone. Probably they were still flying higher and higher in the wind.

Maybe I would see the catalog cats and get to be a good soccer player and have a ride in an airplane and the tallest fig tree in town. And Gloria would be my best friend.

"Gloria," I said, "did you wish we would be friends?"

"You're not supposed to ask me that!" Gloria said.

"I'm sorry," I answered. But inside I was smiling. I guessed one thing Gloria wished for. I was pretty sure we would be friends.

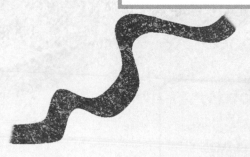

# Dig Deeper

## Use Clues to Analyze the Text

Use these pages to learn about Understanding Characters and Figurative Language. Then read *Gloria Who Might Be My Best Friend* again. Use what you learn to understand it better.

## Understanding Characters

*Gloria Who Might Be My Best Friend* is a story about Julian and his new friend, Gloria. Think about what the characters do, think, and say when things happen in the story. For example, Julian invites Gloria to his house after he meets her. This helps you understand that Julian wants a friend.

As you read, look for text evidence about the characters. List ideas in a chart like this one.

| Character | What Happens | Words, Thoughts, Actions |
|-----------|--------------|--------------------------|
|           |              |                          |

# Figurative Language

Authors sometimes tell how two things are the same using the word *like* or *as*. Sentences that compare using *like* or *as* are called **similes**. Similes help readers to picture story details in their mind. For example, an author may say the moon is like a big, white ball. This helps the reader picture what the moon looks like.

# Your Turn

 **How do friends help each other?** Share your ideas with a small group using text evidence from *Gloria Who Might Be My Best Friend.* Take turns speaking. Use complete sentences when it is your turn to talk.

## Classroom Conversation

Now talk about these questions with the class.

1. How does Julian change because of his new friendship?

2. How can you tell that Julian and Gloria are going to be friends? Use text evidence to explain.

3. What might Julian do the next time a girl wants to be his friend?

ELA RL.2.3, RL.2.7, W.2.1, SL.2.1a, SL.2.6

### WRITE ABOUT READING ............................

**Response** Is Gloria a good friend? Why or why not? Write a paragraph to tell what you think. Use text evidence from the story to explain your answer.

### Writing Tip

Use adjectives to help describe things in your paragraph.

# INFORMATIONAL TEXT

☑ **GENRE**

**Informational text** gives facts about a topic. This is from a how-to book.

☑ **TEXT FOCUS**

**Directions** tell how to do or make something step-by-step.

# How to Make a Kite

**by Joanna Korba**

Can you feel lonely flying a kite? If you answered no, you guessed right!

If you take kite flying seriously, you will want to make your own kite. The first step in planning your kite is to read all of these directions. You may want to copy them onto another sheet of paper first.

# Directions

## Materials

**2 sticks with small cuts on both ends**

24 inches

18 inches

**string**

**colored paper**

**glue and scissors**

**5 pieces of ribbon**

## What to Do

**1** First, make a cross with the sticks. Tie a string around the middle.

**2** Run string around the edge to make a frame. Tie it tightly at the top end. Then cut the string.

**3** Lay the kite frame on the paper. Cut the paper so that it is slightly larger than the kite frame.

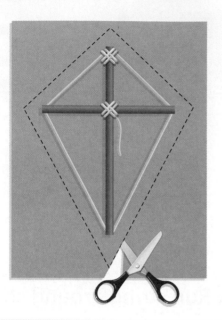

**4** Fold the paper over the kite frame. Glue it down. Then tie a long string to the middle of the frame.

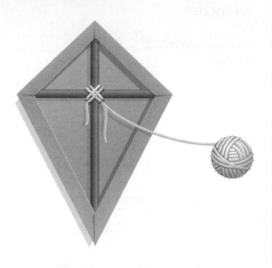

**5** Cut a piece of string 36 inches long and make the tail. Tie a ribbon to the string every 6 inches with a tight knot. Too many ribbons will make your kite fly heavily.

# Compare Texts

## TEXT TO TEXT

**Talk About Directions** Look back at how Gloria and Julian make their kite in the story. Then look at the directions for making a kite in *How to Make a Kite*. Which would be more helpful if you wanted to make a kite? Share your ideas with a partner.

## TEXT TO SELF

**Talk About Making Friends** What does Julian do to make Gloria his friend? What do you do when trying to make a new friend? Share your ideas with a partner.

## TEXT TO WORLD

**Connect to Social Studies** Think of something you know how to make. Tell the directions to a partner. Have your partner ask questions to better understand the steps. Then ask your partner to retell the directions.

ELA RL.2.1, RL.2.7, SL.2.3, SL.2.4

# Grammar

**Using Adjectives** Add -*er* to **adjectives** to compare two people, animals, places, or things. Add -*est* to compare more than two people, animals, places, or things.

| Comparing Two | Comparing More Than Two |
|---|---|
| Lee is taller than Kim. Maine is smaller than Florida. | Lee is the tallest boy in class. Rhode Island is the smallest state. |

**Try This!** **Work with a partner to choose the correct adjective for each sentence. Then read the sentences aloud.**

❶ I am (older, oldest) than my friend.

❷ Main Street is the (longer, longest) street in town.

❸ A kite flies (higher, highest) than a paper plane.

❹ Gloria can do the (faster, fastest) cartwheels of all.

270    ELA L.2.1e

In your writing, use adjectives that compare to tell more about nouns. Add *-er* or *-est* to adjectives to compare two or more people, animals, places, or things.

## Sentence That Does Not Tell Enough

Florian has a new kite.

## Sentences That Tell More

Florian has a newer kite than Meg has.
Dan has the newest kite on the block.

## Connect Grammar to Writing

**When you revise your paragraphs that compare and contrast, add *-er* or *-est* to adjectives to tell your reader more.**

# Informative Writing

✓**Evidence** When you write to **compare and contrast,** connect details to the main idea.

Leo wrote a draft to compare and contrast himself with his cousin. Later, he revised his draft to be sure his details connect to the main idea of each paragraph.

## Revised Draft

My cousin Anthony and I are like twins. We are both the same age. We are about the same height. Anthony wears glasses, but I don't. I love scary movies, and so does he. We both like writing stories.

Even though we are alike in many ways, we are also different.

# My Cousin and Me
## by Leo Saint-Clair

My cousin Anthony and I are like twins. We are both the same age. We are about the same height. I love scary movies, and so does he. We both like writing stories.

Even though we are alike in many ways, we are also different. Anthony wears glasses, but I don't. He's a great swimmer. I play chess. He loves loud music, and I love animals. Even with our differences, we always have fun together!

## Reading as a Writer

What did Leo move to make sure his details connect to the right paragraph's main idea? Are your details in the right paragraph?

I put details in one paragraph to compare and details in the other to contrast.

THE GOAT
IN THE RUG

As told to Charles L. Blood & Martin Link
BY GERALDINE

Illustrated by
Nancy Winslow Parker

**Basket Weaving**

Q **LANGUAGE DETECTIVE**

**Talk About Words**
Work with a partner. Use the Vocabulary words in new sentences that tell about the photos. Write the sentences.

# Vocabulary in Context

▶ Read each **Context Card**.

▶ Talk about a picture. Use a different Vocabulary word from the one on the card.

**1**

### yarn

People use yarn to knit sweaters, hats, and mittens.

**2**

### strands

The strands of yarn are tied into knots at the bottom of this rug.

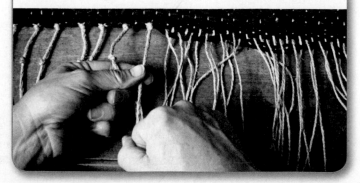

### 3 spinning

It takes a lot of practice spinning chunks of wool into thin yarn.

### 4 dye

These shirts are soaked in dye to make them colorful.

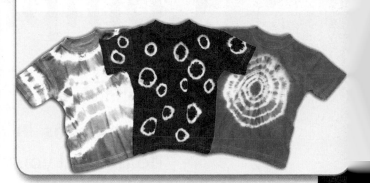

### 5 weave

This woman will weave dried grasses into baskets.

### 6 sharpening

This pencil does not need sharpening anymore!

### 7 duplicated

Some colors on this rug are duplicated. They appear again and again.

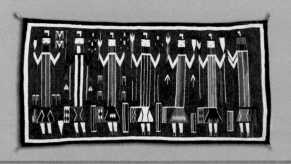

### 8 delicious

This baker makes delicious cakes. They are very tasty!

# Read and Comprehend

**TARGET SKILL**

**Conclusions** In *The Goat in the Rug*, the authors do not tell you everything you need to know. Ask questions about details in the words and pictures. Looking for text evidence will help you make a smart guess about what is happening. Making a smart guess is called drawing a **conclusion.**

A chart like this can help you record details and conclusions.

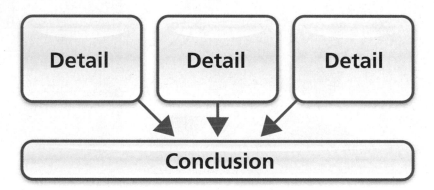

✓ **TARGET STRATEGY**

**Summarize** As you read, stop to tell the most important ideas in your own words.

ELA RI.2.1, RI.2.7, SL.2.1a

## Visual Arts

Visual art is art that you look at, like a drawing or a sculpture. Artists use different things to make visual art. Some use paint to create their art. Others use metal, wood, or clay. Even yarn can be used to create art.

In *The Goat in the Rug*, you will learn about the art of weaving a rug. The artist in the selection uses yarn to make colorful patterns in her rugs.

### 💬 Talk About It

Think about a time when you made a piece of art. How did you feel when you were making it? What did you like best about it? Describe your feelings to the class. Take turns speaking, and listen carefully when others are speaking.

# ANCHOR TEXT

THE GOAT
IN THE RUG

As told to Charles L. Blood & Martin Link
BY GERALDINE

Illustrated by
Nancy Winslow Parker

## ✅ GENRE

**Narrative nonfiction** tells a true story about a topic. As you read, look for:

- ▸ a setting that is real
- ▸ events in time order
- ▸ facts and information

**MEET THE AUTHORS**

## Charles L. Blood and Martin Link

These two authors wrote *The Goat in the Rug* from the point of view of Geraldine, the goat. Charles L. Blood also wrote a book about Native American crafts and games. Martin Link was once a ranger with the National Park Service in Arizona.

**MEET THE ILLUSTRATOR**

## Nancy Winslow Parker

When Nancy Winslow Parker was a kid, she looked forward to spring cleaning. That was when her mom put new shelf paper in the kitchen cabinets and dresser drawers. The lucky young artist was given all the old paper to draw on!

# THE GOAT IN THE RUG

## BY GERALDINE

as told to Charles L. Blood and Martin Link

illustrated by Nancy Winslow Parker

**ESSENTIAL QUESTION**

How is art connected to the past?

My name is Geraldine and I live near a place called Window Rock with my Navajo friend, Glenmae. It's called Window Rock because it has a big round hole in it that looks like a window open to the sky.

Glenmae is called Glenmae most of the time because it's easier to say than her Indian name: Glee 'Nasbah. In English that means something like female warrior, but she's really a Navajo weaver. I guess that's why, one day, she decided to weave me into a rug.

I remember it was a warm, sunny afternoon.
Glenmae had spent most of the morning sharpening a
large pair of scissors. I had no idea what she was going
to use them for, but it didn't take me long to find out.

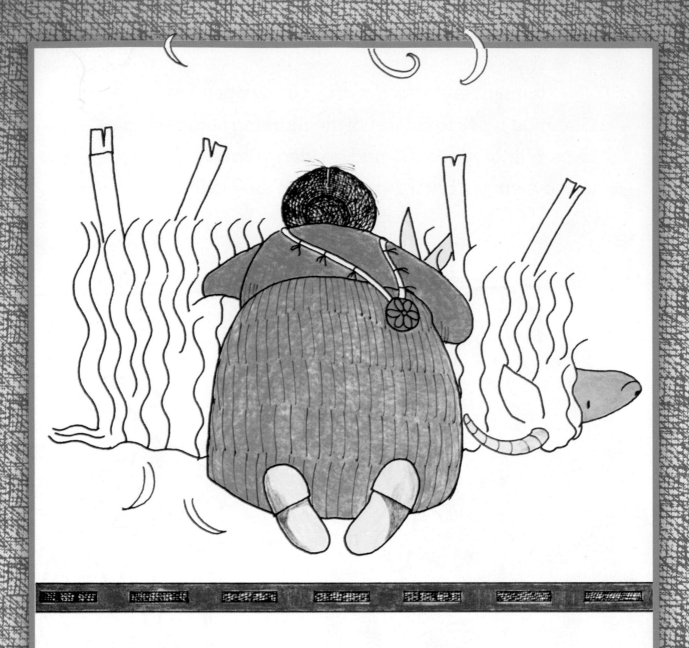

Before I knew what was happening, I was on the ground and Glenmae was clipping off my wool in great long strands. (It's called mohair, really.) It didn't hurt at all, but I admit I kicked up my heels some. I'm very ticklish for a goat.

I might have looked a little naked and silly afterwards, but my, did I feel nice and cool! So I decided to stick around and see what would happen next.

The first thing Glenmae did was chop up roots from a yucca plant. The roots made a soapy, rich lather when she mixed them with water.

She washed my wool in the suds until it was clean and white.

After that, a little bit of me (you might say) was hung up in the sun to dry. When my wool was dry, Glenmae took out two large square combs with many teeth.

By combing my wool between these carding combs, as they're called, she removed any bits of twigs or burrs and straightened out the fibers. She told me it helped make a smoother yarn for spinning.

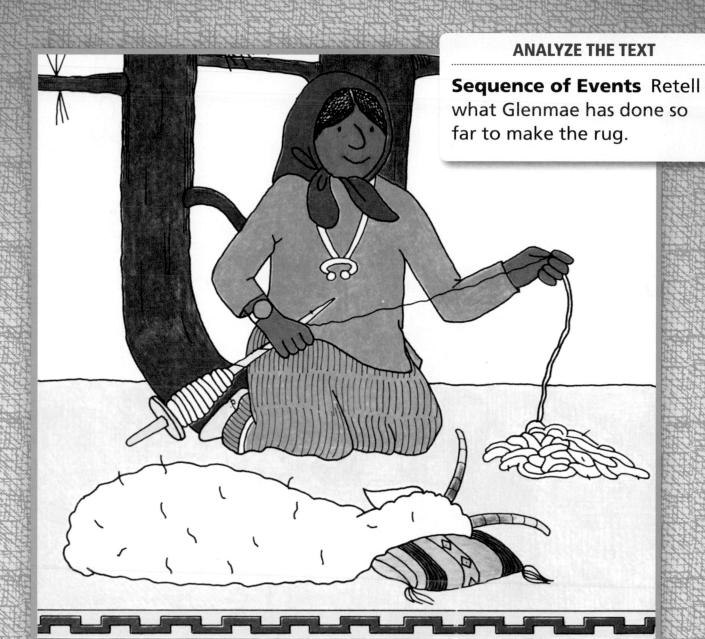

**ANALYZE THE TEXT**

**Sequence of Events** Retell what Glenmae has done so far to make the rug.

Then, Glenmae carefully started to spin my wool—one small bundle at a time—into yarn. I was beginning to find out it takes a long while to make a Navajo rug.

Again and again, Glenmae twisted and pulled, twisted and pulled the wool. Then she spun it around a long, thin stick she called a spindle. As she twisted and pulled and spun, the finer, stronger and smoother the yarn became.

A few days later, Glenmae and I went for a walk. She said we were going to find some special plants she would use to make dye.

I didn't know what "dye" meant, but it sounded like a picnic to me. I do love to eat plants. That's what got me into trouble.

While Glenmae was out looking for more plants, I ate every one she had already collected in her bucket. Delicious!

The next day, Glenmae made me stay home
while she walked miles to a store. She said the dye
she could buy wasn't the same as the kind she makes
from plants, but since I'd made such a pig of myself, it
would have to do.

I was really worried that she would still be angry with me when she got back. She wasn't, though, and pretty soon she had three big potfuls of dye boiling over a fire.

Then I saw what Glenmae had meant by dyeing. She dipped my white wool into one pot . . . and it turned pink! She dipped it in again. It turned a darker pink! By the time she'd finished dipping it in and out and hung it up to dry, it was a beautiful deep red.

After that, she dyed some of my wool brown, and some of it black. I couldn't help wondering if those plants I'd eaten would turn all of me the same colors.

While I was worrying about that, Glenmae started
to make our rug. She took a ball of yarn and wrapped
it around and around two poles. I lost count when she'd
reached three hundred wraps. I guess I was too busy
thinking about what it would be like to be the only red,
white, black, and brown goat at Window Rock.

It wasn't long before Glenmae had finished wrapping. Then she hung the poles with the yarn on a big wooden frame. It looked like a picture frame made of logs—she called it a "loom."

After a whole week of getting ready to weave, Glenmae started. She began weaving at the bottom of the loom. Then, one strand of yarn at a time, our rug started growing toward the top.

A few strands of black. A few of brown. A few of red. In and out. Back and forth. Until, in a few days, the pattern of our rug was clear to see.

Our rug grew very slowly. Just as every Navajo weaver before her had done for hundreds and hundreds of years, Glenmae formed a design that would never be duplicated.

Then, at last, the weaving was finished! But not
until I'd checked it quite thoroughly in front and in back,
did I let Glenmae take our rug off the loom.

There was a lot of me in that rug. I wanted it to be perfect. And it was.

Since then, my wool has grown almost long enough for Glenmae and me to make another rug. I hope we do very soon. Because, you see, there aren't too many weavers like Glenmae left among the Navajos.

And there's only one goat like me, Geraldine.

This is the true
story of a weaver
and her goat who
lived in the Navajo
Nation at Window
Rock, Arizona.

# Dig Deeper

## Use Clues to Analyze the Text

Use these pages to learn about Conclusions and Sequence of Events. Then read *The Goat in the Rug* again. Use what you learn to understand it better.

## Conclusions

*The Goat in the Rug* explains how some rugs are made. As you read, ask yourself questions to draw **conclusions** about what the authors do not say. For example, you might ask why or how something happens. Look for text evidence in the words or pictures to help you answer the question. Then draw a conclusion.

Use a chart like the one below to help you draw conclusions about what the authors want you to know.

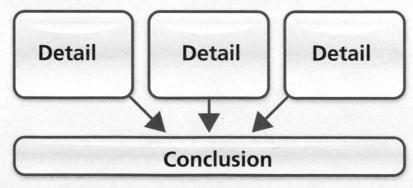

## Sequence of Events

Glenmae follows many steps to weave her rug. She must complete one step before doing the next one. She does the steps in order, or the rug will not turn out right. Think about what she does first, next, and last.

# Your Turn

 **How is art connected to the past?** Discuss your ideas with a partner. Be sure to give examples from the text evidence in *The Goat in the Rug*. Take turns speaking and listening. Add your own ideas to what your partner says.

## Classroom Conversation

Now talk about these questions with the class.

1 Which pictures help you understand what the authors do not tell you?

2 What do you think would be the hardest step in making a Navajo rug? Why?

3 Why is it important for Glenmae to do each step in order?

### WRITE ABOUT READING

**Response** What steps does Glenmae take to make the rug? Draw each step. Then write the steps below the pictures. Use text evidence to help you list the steps correctly.

## Writing Tip

Use words such as *first, then, after that,* and *finally* to help tell the steps in order.

## INFORMATIONAL TEXT

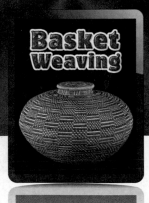

### ✅ GENRE

**Informational text** gives facts about a topic. This is a magazine article.

### ✅ TEXT FOCUS

**Directions** help readers understand how to make or do something. As you read, pay attention to how one step allows the next step to happen.

# Basket Weaving

### by Becky Manfredini

## A Native American Tradition

Some Native Americans weave beautiful baskets in many shapes and sizes. Some are for storing delicious foods. Others are to store clothes in. Some baskets are even used for carrying water! Basket makers make baskets for themselves and to sell.

## Gathering Materials

Rug weavers have to make the material they use to weave rugs by spinning wool into yarn. Basket makers use strands of willow or special grasses to weave their baskets. After sharpening their cutting tools, basket makers go to places where the materials grow and cut off as much as they need.

Weaving is a tradition. Mothers teach their daughters how to weave.

## How to Weave a Basket

Basket makers prepare the willow strands by soaking them in water. That makes them soft and easy to bend. It makes the strands much easier to weave. Then they weave the strands into a pattern.

Basket makers use dye they make from plants to make their baskets colorful. No basket is just like any other basket. The patterns are never duplicated. It takes a lot of skill to weave a beautiful basket.

**The weaver holds thin strips of willow tightly as she works on this type of basket.**

# Compare Texts

## TEXT TO TEXT

**Talk About Topics** How are the *The Goat in the Rug* and *Basket Weaving* the same? How are they different? Think about which has only facts and which has facts and made-up events. Talk with a small group. Use text evidence from the selections to help you answer.

## TEXT TO SELF

**Discuss a Skill** What tools does Glenmae use to make the rug? Think of something you know how to do. Explain to a partner the tools you need for your skill. Tell how to use them.

## TEXT TO WORLD

**Connect to Social Studies** Today, many rugs are made by machines instead of by hand. Look up some other things people used to make by hand.

ELA RI.2.2, RI.2.9, W.2.8, SL.2.4

# Grammar

**Irregular Verbs** The **verbs** *have* and *has* can be used to tell what someone has right now. The verb *had* can be used to tell what someone had in the past. The verbs *do* and *does* can be used to tell what someone does right now. The verb *did* can be used to tell what someone did in the past.

| Now | In the Past |
|---|---|
| I have a goat. | I had a goat when I was young. |
| She has a goat. | She had a goat a year ago. |
| We do nice work. | We did nice work yesterday. |
| He does nice work. | He did nice work last week. |

 **Choose the correct verb to complete each sentence. Then write the sentence correctly.**

❶ He (has, had) a loom now.

❷ I (do, did) many crafts last year.

❸ They (has, had) yarn before.

When you write, make sure you use the right form for the verbs in your sentences. The verb should match the subject of the sentence.

| Wrong | Right |
|---|---|
| My uncle **have** many rugs in his store.<br>Last month, I **does** some work for him. | My uncle **has** many rugs in his store.<br>Last month, I **did** some work for him. |

## Connect Grammar to Writing

**When you edit your writing, check to see if you have used the correct form for each verb.**

# Informative Writing

**☑ Elaboration** When you write, try not to repeat the same word too many times. Use synonyms instead. Synonyms are words that mean the same thing.

Kenny wrote an **informational paragraph** telling how Glenmae weaves a rug. Later, Kenny revised his draft by replacing some of the repeated words with synonyms.

## Writing Checklist

☑ **Purpose**
Did I include important information?

☑ **Organization**
Did I tell the steps in order?

☑ **Elaboration**
Did I use synonyms to avoid repeating words?

☑ **Conventions**
Did I capitalize and punctuate my sentences correctly?

## Revised Draft

Glenmae has a special way of making yarn. First, she cuts the wool. She ~~cuts~~ clips off her goat's hair using scissors. Then she ~~cuts~~ chops up roots from a yucca plant.

# How Glenmae Makes Yarn
## by Kenny Hutchins

Glenmae has a special way of making yarn. First, she cuts the wool. She clips off her goat's hair using scissors. Then she chops up roots from a yucca plant. She mixes the roots with water. She uses this to wash the goat's hair. When the hair is dry, she uses two combs to straighten it. Then she twists and pulls the wool around a spindle. She does this many times until strong yarn is made.

## Reading as a Writer

How did using many different words make Kenny's writing better? Where can you replace words with synonyms in your own paper?

In my final paper, I replaced some repeated words with synonyms.

## 🔍 LANGUAGE DETECTIVE

**Talk About Words**
Work with a partner.
Choose one of the
sentences. Take out
the Vocabulary word.
Put in a word that
means the same or
almost the same thing.
Tell how the sentences
are the same and how
they are different.

# Vocabulary
## in Context

▶ Read each **Context Card.**

▶ Ask a question that uses
one of the Vocabulary
words.

**1** **tumbling**
This acrobat is tumbling
through the air.

**2** **flung**
When something is flung, it
is thrown with force.

### 3 tangled

These pieces of string are tangled. It is hard to separate them.

### 4 empty

This pot is empty. There is nothing in it.

### 5 swift

Swift horses move very fast.

### 6 peacefully

The farm animals are sleeping peacefully. Nothing is bothering them.

### 7 stream

This stream flows into a larger river.

### 8 blazed

A forest fire blazed, or burned brightly, for many hours.

# Read and Comprehend

✅ **TARGET SKILL**

**Cause and Effect** In *Half-Chicken*, some events cause other events to happen. The first event is the **cause**. The second event is the **effect**.

To figure out how the events might be connected, ask yourself what happens and why. Look for text evidence in the words and pictures to help you find the answers. Use a chart like the one below to list causes and effects in a story.

| Cause | Effect |
|-------|--------|
|       |        |

✅ **TARGET STRATEGY**

**Visualize** As you read, picture what is happening to help you understand and remember important ideas and details.

ELA RL.2.1, RL.2.2, RL.2.7, SL.2.1a

## Traditional Stories

People have been telling traditional stories, or folktales, for many years. Folktales often tell about events that could not happen in real life.

Characters in folktales often learn a lesson. A folktale may also explain why something is the way it is. In *Half-Chicken,* you will read about an important lesson that the main character learns.

### 💬 Think | Pair | Share

Think about why authors of folktales might use animals as characters. Share your ideas with a partner. Take turns speaking, and listen carefully to each other. Then share your ideas with the class.

# ANCHOR TEXT

☑ **GENRE**

A **folktale** is a kind of traditional tale. As you read, look for:
▸ a simple plot that teaches a lesson
▸ animal characters who talk and act like people

**MEET THE AUTHOR**

## Alma Flor Ada

Alma Flor Ada comes from a family of storytellers. She first heard the story of Half-Chicken from her grandmother. It was one of her favorites as a child. She loved the folktale so much that she decided to write her own retelling of it.

**MEET THE ILLUSTRATOR**

## Kim Howard

Kim Howard has illustrated more than twenty-five children's books. Her style is full of color and detail. When she is not illustrating, she is painting and making collages. She also teaches students all over the world about art.

# HALF-CHICKEN

by Alma Flor Ada
illustrated by Kim Howard

Have you ever seen a weather vane? Do you know why there is a little rooster on one end, spinning around to let us know which way the wind is blowing?

Well, I'll tell you. It's an old, old story that my grandmother once told me. And before that, her grandmother told it to her. It goes like this . . .

316

A long, long time ago, on a Mexican ranch, a mother hen was sitting on her eggs. One by one, the baby chicks began to hatch, leaving their empty shells behind. One, two, three, four . . . twelve chicks had hatched. But the last egg still had not cracked open.

The hen did not know what to do. The chicks were running here and there, and she could not chase after them because she was still sitting on the last egg.

Finally there was a tiny sound. The baby chick was pecking at its egg from the inside. The hen quickly helped it break open the shell, and at last the thirteenth chick came out into the world.

Yet this was no ordinary chick. He had only one wing, only one leg, only one eye, and only half as many feathers as the other chicks.

It was not long before everyone at the ranch
knew that a very special chick had been born.
The ducks told the turkeys. The turkeys told
the pigeons. The pigeons told the swallows. And
the swallows flew over the fields, spreading the
news to the cows grazing peacefully with their
calves, the fierce bulls and the swift horses.

Soon the hen was surrounded by animals who wanted to see the strange chick.

One of the ducks said, "But he only has one wing!"

And one of the turkeys added, "Why, he's only a . . . half chicken!"

From then on, everyone called him Half-Chicken. And Half-Chicken, finding himself at the center of all this attention, became very vain.

One day he overheard the swallows, who traveled a great deal, talking about him: "Not even at the court of the viceroy in Mexico City is there anyone so unique."

Then Half-Chicken decided that it was time for him to leave the ranch. Early one morning he said his farewells, announcing:

*"Good-bye, good-bye!*
*I'm off to Mexico City*
*to see the court of the viceroy!"*

And *hip hop hip hop*, off he went, hippety-hopping along on his only foot.

**ANALYZE THE TEXT**

**Cause and Effect** Why does Half-Chicken leave the ranch?

Half-Chicken had not walked very far when he found a stream whose waters were blocked by some branches.

"Good morning, Half-Chicken. Would you please move the branches that are blocking my way?" asked the stream.

Half-Chicken moved the branches aside. But when the stream suggested that he stay awhile and take a swim, he answered:

*"I have no time to lose.*
*I'm off to Mexico City*
*to see the court of the viceroy!"*

And *hip hop hip hop*, off he went, hippety-hopping along on his only foot.

A little while later, Half-Chicken found a small fire burning between some rocks. The fire was almost out.

"Good morning, Half-Chicken. Please, fan me a little with your wing, for I am about to go out," asked the fire.

Half-Chicken fanned the fire with his wing, and it blazed up again. But when the fire suggested that he stay awhile and warm up, he answered:

*"I have no time to lose.*
*I'm off to Mexico City*
*to see the court of the viceroy!"*

And *hip hop hip hop*, off he went, hippety-hopping along on his only foot.

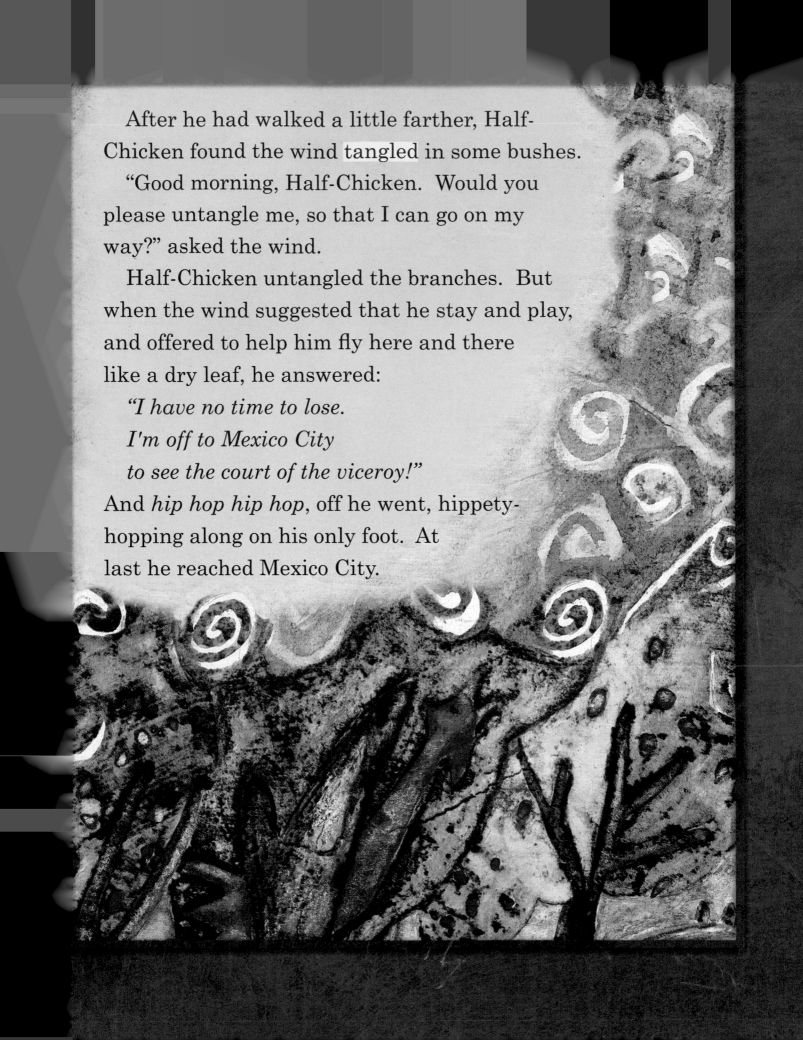

After he had walked a little farther, Half-Chicken found the wind tangled in some bushes.

"Good morning, Half-Chicken. Would you please untangle me, so that I can go on my way?" asked the wind.

Half-Chicken untangled the branches. But when the wind suggested that he stay and play, and offered to help him fly here and there like a dry leaf, he answered:

*"I have no time to lose.*
*I'm off to Mexico City*
*to see the court of the viceroy!"*

And *hip hop hip hop*, off he went, hippety-hopping along on his only foot. At last he reached Mexico City.

Half-Chicken crossed the enormous Great Plaza. He passed the stalls laden with meat, fish, vegetables, fruit, cheese, and honey. He passed the Parián, the market where all kinds of beautiful goods were sold. Finally, he reached the gate of the viceroy's palace.

"Good afternoon," said Half-Chicken to the guards in fancy uniforms who stood in front of the palace. "I've come to see the viceroy."

One of the guards began to laugh. The other one said, "You'd better go in around the back and through the kitchen."

So Half-Chicken went, *hip hop hip hop*, around the palace and to the kitchen door.

**ANALYZE THE TEXT**

**Point of View** How does the cook feel about using Half-Chicken in the soup? How does Half-Chicken feel about it?

The cook who saw him said, "What luck! This chicken is just what I need to make a soup for the vicereine." And he threw Half-Chicken into a kettle of water that was sitting on the fire.

When Half-Chicken felt how hot the water was, he said, "Oh fire, help me! Please, don't burn me!"

327

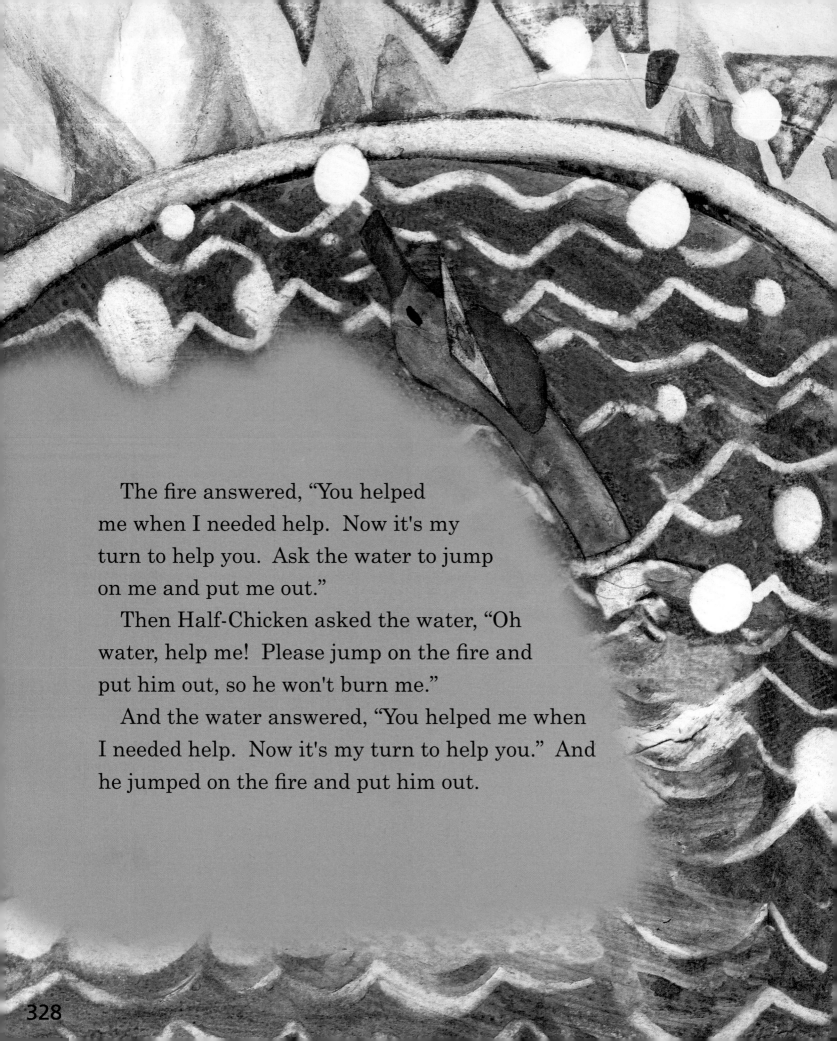

The fire answered, "You helped
me when I needed help. Now it's my
turn to help you. Ask the water to jump
on me and put me out."

Then Half-Chicken asked the water, "Oh
water, help me! Please jump on the fire and
put him out, so he won't burn me."

And the water answered, "You helped me when
I needed help. Now it's my turn to help you." And
he jumped on the fire and put him out.

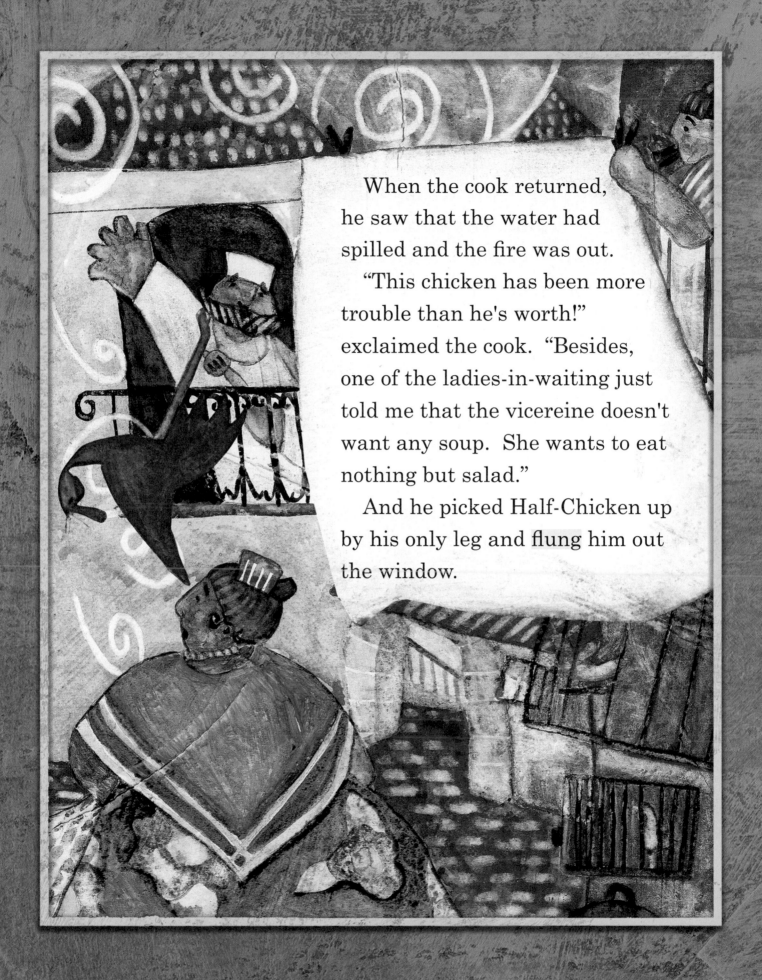

When the cook returned, he saw that the water had spilled and the fire was out.

"This chicken has been more trouble than he's worth!" exclaimed the cook. "Besides, one of the ladies-in-waiting just told me that the vicereine doesn't want any soup. She wants to eat nothing but salad."

And he picked Half-Chicken up by his only leg and flung him out the window.

When Half-Chicken was tumbling through the air, he called out: "Oh wind, help me, please!"

And the wind answered, "You helped me when I needed help. Now it's my turn to help you."

And the wind blew fiercely. He lifted Half-Chicken higher and higher, until the little rooster landed on one of the towers of the palace.

"From there you can see everything you want, Half-Chicken, with no danger of ending up in the cooking pot."

And from that day on, weathercocks have stood on their only leg, seeing everything that happens below, and pointing whichever way their friend the wind blows.

# Dig Deeper

## Use Clues to Analyze the Text

Use these pages to learn about Cause and Effect and Point of View. Then read *Half-Chicken* again. Use what you learn to understand it better.

## Cause and Effect

In *Half-Chicken*, one event often makes another event happen. When the cook puts Half-Chicken in hot water over a fire, Half-Chicken asks the fire not to burn him. Being put in the hot water is the **cause.** Asking the fire for help is the **effect.**

As you read, ask yourself what happens and why. Use text evidence from the words and pictures to help you answer. You can fill in a chart to list causes and effects.

| Cause | Effect |
|-------|--------|
|       |        |

**ELA** RL.2.1, RL.2.6, RL.2.7

# Point of View

Characters in a story sometimes think about the same event in different ways. Each character has a different **point of view.** As you read a story aloud, think about how the characters feel about what is happening. Think about why they say what they say. Use a different voice for each character to show how the character feels.

# Your Turn

**Why are some stories told over and over again?**
Think about *Half-Chicken*. What makes this an important story to tell? Use words and pictures from the story to help you answer. Talk about your ideas with a partner. Ask questions if you need to better understand your partner's ideas.

## Classroom Conversation

Now talk about these questions with the class.

1. What might have happened if Half-Chicken had not helped fire, water, and wind?

2. How do you think Half-Chicken feels at the end of the story? Use text evidence to help you explain.

3. How can you tell that this is a folktale?

### WRITE ABOUT READING

**Response** Half-Chicken was very vain. However, he also showed that he could be thoughtful of others. Think of the ways Half-Chicken was thoughtful and helpful. Write a paragraph to explain ways he was helpful. Use text evidence from the story. Write an opening sentence to begin your paragraph. Write a closing sentence at the end.

## Writing Tip

Use the correct end mark at the end of each sentence.

✅ **GENRE**

**Traditional tales** are stories that have been told for many years. This traditional tale is a fable.

✅ **TEXT FOCUS**

A **moral** of a fable is the lesson that a character learns. As you read, think of what the moral of this fable might be.

# The Lion and the Mouse

Once a lion was sleeping peacefully in the grass. Then a mouse ran up his tail. The lion woke up. He grabbed the mouse and flung it. The mouse went tumbling across the ground.

"Please don't eat me," the mouse cried. "I promise that I will help you one day if you let me go."

"You help me?" the lion laughed. "I will let you go because you are so funny!"

Later, the lion was having a drink at a stream. He saw that a campfire blazed across the way. The camp was empty.

"Hunters must be near," he said. Just then a net fell on him. The lion was tangled in it. He roared with all his might.

Suddenly, the mouse appeared. "I will get you out in no time."

The swift mouse nibbled at the net. Soon, the lion was free.

"I didn't believe you could help me," said the lion. "You saved my life."

"It was simply my turn to help you," said the mouse.

# Compare Texts

**Compare and Contrast** With a partner, retell the main events of *Half-Chicken* and *The Lion and the Mouse*. Then tell the lesson learned in each. Talk about how the lessons are the same and different.

**Tell a Moral Story** Think about how Half-Chicken and the mouse helped others. When have you helped someone? Write a paragraph to tell about how you helped.

**Connect to Art** Work with a small group to think of your own weather vane using an animal that is not a chicken. Draw a picture of what the weather vane would look like.

ELA RL.2.2, W.2.8

339

# Grammar

**Irregular Action Verbs** The **verbs** *run, come, see,* and *go* name an action that is happening now. Do not add *-ed* to these verbs to tell what happened in the past. Instead use *ran, came, saw,* and *went.*

| What Is Happening Now | What Happened in the Past |
|---|---|
| I run down the road. | I ran down the road yesterday. |
| People come to the farm to look at the chicken. | People came to the farm to look at the chicken last fall. |
| They see the rain falling. | Yesterday, they saw the rain falling. |
| We go to the plaza. | We went to the plaza last year. |

 **Read each sentence aloud. Change each underlined verb to tell what happened in the past.**

❶ I <u>run</u> past a farm with a weather vane.

❷ I <u>come</u> back for my friend Mike.

❸ We <u>see</u> the chicken.

❹ The weather vanes <u>go</u> around and around.

When you write, use exact verbs. They make your sentences interesting and tell your reader more about what is happening.

| Without Exact Verb | With Exact Verb |
|---|---|
| The chicken went down the road. | The chicken tumbled down the road. |

| Verb | Exact Verbs |
|---|---|
| run | race, zoom, dash, speed |
| see | spot, watch, view, spy |
| go | move, chase, leave, flee |
| come | near, enter, reach, arrive |

## Connect Grammar to Writing

When you revise your research report next week, look for any verbs that you can change to more exact verbs.

# Informative Writing

☑ **Evidence**  When you write a **research report,** you can use a K-W-L chart to help you plan your writing.

Rosa started with a K-W-L chart on giraffes. She made notes about what she learned. She added more details. Finally, she put the information in order.

## Exploring a Topic

| What I Know | What I Want to Know | What I Learned |
|---|---|---|
| Giraffes are wild animals. | Where they live | Grasslands of Africa |
| Giraffes are tall. | How tall are they? | Tallest animals 18 feet |
| They have long necks. | What do they eat? | Eat acacia leaves Get water from leaves |

### Writing Process Checklist

▶ **Prewrite**
☑ **Did I choose an interesting topic?**
☑ **Did I do research to answer my questions?**
☑ **Did I come up with details that will inform the reader about my topic?**
**Draft**
**Revise**
**Edit**
**Publish and Share**

## Flow Chart

Giraffes live on the grasslands of Africa.

↓

They are 18 feet tall with long necks, spots, and hairy horns.

↓

They eat acacia leaves, which also give them water.

↓

Lions, crocodiles, hyenas, and wild dogs are their enemies.

↓

Giraffes stay together, watch for enemies, and are fast.

## Reading as a Writer

**What did Rosa add to her K-W-L chart? How did she organize her information? How will you organize your information?**

I put the information I learned in an order that makes sense.

FROM SEED TO PLANT
BY GAIL GIBBONS

SUPER SOIL

## 🔍 LANGUAGE DETECTIVE

**Talk About Words**
**Nouns** are words that name people, places, animals, or things. Work with a partner. Find the Vocabulary words that are nouns. What are your clues? Use the nouns in new sentences.

# Vocabulary in Context

▶ Read each **Context Card**.

▶ Place the Vocabulary words in alphabetical order.

---

**1**
### grain
It is hard to pick up only one small grain of rice.

---

**2**
### pod
A pod, or shell, protects peas as they grow.

### 3 soak

The children **soak** the soil with water to help the seeds grow.

### 4 soften

The boiling water will **soften** the noodles.

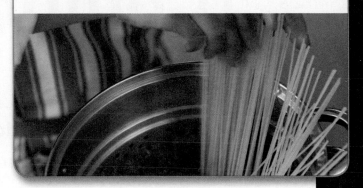

### 5 root

The **root** of this plant goes deep into the soil.

### 6 shoot

We planted seeds in the ground. Later, we saw a **shoot** begin to grow.

### 7 nutrition

Eating vegetables is a good way to get the **nutrition** that your body needs.

### 8 tasty

I ate the whole apple because it was so **tasty**!

FROM SEED TO PLANT
BY GAIL GIBBONS

# Read and Comprehend

**Text and Graphic Features** An author often includes text and graphic features to help the reader understand more about the text. Labels are an example of a **text feature.** Pictures, charts, and diagrams are examples of **graphic features.**

You can use a chart like the one below to list the types of features you find in a selection. Then you can tell why you think the author used each one.

| Text or Graphic Feature | Page Number | Purpose |
|---|---|---|
|  |  |  |

**Monitor/Clarify** Stop and think when you don't understand something. Find text evidence to help you figure out what doesn't make sense.

## Life Cycles

When you look up at a giant tree, it is hard to imagine that it was once a tiny seed. It was, though! The seed was in the ground. Sunlight and rain helped it to grow. The tree was small at first, but then it grew and grew. After years of growing, it became a full-grown tree. When seeds fall from the tree, more trees will grow. This is the tree's life cycle.

Many plants grow this same way. You will read more about how plants grow in *From Seed to Plant*.

### Think | Draw | Pair | Share

Think about what you just read. What do you think the stages of the life cycle of a tree look like? Draw a picture of the different stages. Share your drawings with a partner. Then share your drawings with the class. How are the drawings alike? How are they different?

# ANCHOR TEXT

FROM SEED TO PLANT
BY GAIL GIBBONS

☑ **GENRE**

**Informational text** gives facts about a topic. As you read, look for:

▶ pictures and labels
▶ facts and details
▶ diagrams that help explain the topic

**MEET THE AUTHOR AND ILLUSTRATOR**
## Gail Gibbons

Gail Gibbons was a very curious child. Her parents say that she always asked a lot of questions. She also loved to draw and paint. One of her first jobs was doing artwork for a children's television show. After that she wrote her first book. Since then she has written more than 135 informational books! She loves her job because she still likes to ask questions. She finds the answers and then writes about them in her books.

# FROM SEED TO PLANT

## by Gail Gibbons

**TULIP** **DAISY** **CORN** **PEA** **ROSE** **BUTTERCUP**

Most plants make seeds. A seed contains the beginning of a new plant. Seeds are different shapes, sizes and colors. All seeds grow into the same kind of plant that made them.

Many plants grow flowers. Flowers are where most seeds begin.

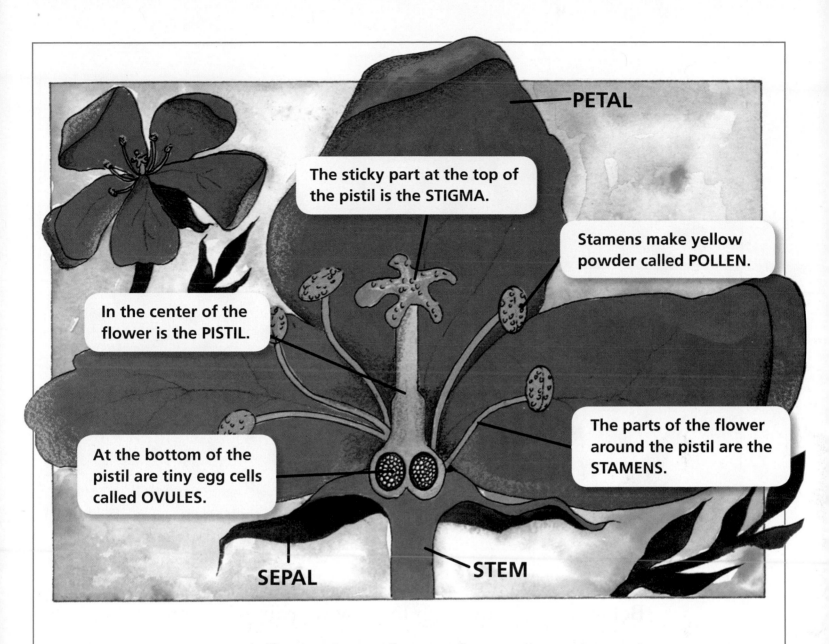

PETAL

The sticky part at the top of the pistil is the STIGMA.

Stamens make yellow powder called POLLEN.

In the center of the flower is the PISTIL.

The parts of the flower around the pistil are the STAMENS.

At the bottom of the pistil are tiny egg cells called OVULES.

SEPAL

STEM

A flower is made up of many parts.

**ANALYZE THE TEXT**

**Text and Graphic Features** How does the diagram of the flower help you better understand the information on this page?

Before a seed can begin to grow, a grain of pollen from the stamen must land on the stigma at the top of the pistil of a flower like itself. This is called pollination.

Pollination happens in different ways. Often, wind blows pollen from flower to flower.

Bees, other insects and hummingbirds help pollinate, too. While they visit flowers for their sweet juice, called nectar, pollen rubs onto their bodies. Then they carry the pollen to another flower where it comes off onto its pistil.

If a pollen grain from a flower lands on the pistil of the same kind of flower, it grows a long tube through the pistil into an ovule. This is the beginning of a seed.

The seeds grow inside the flower, even as the flower begins to die. As the seeds become bigger, a fruit or pod grows around them. The fruit or pod protects the seeds.

When the fruit or pod ripens, it breaks open.
The seeds are ready to become new plants.

Some seeds fall to the ground around the base
of the plant where they will grow. Some pods or
fruits open and the seeds pop out. Sometimes,
when birds eat berries, they drop the seeds.

Other seeds fall into streams, ponds, rivers or the ocean. There, they travel on the water until they stick to dirt along a shore.

The wind scatters seeds. Some seeds have fluff on them that lets them float to the ground like tiny parachutes. Others have wings that spin as they fall.

Animals help scatter seeds, too. They hide acorns and nuts in the ground. Some seeds have hooks that stick to the fur of animals or people's clothes. Later, they drop off onto the ground.

A flower bed or vegetable garden is beautiful! Seeds are planted to grow in the gardens. The seeds come in small envelopes or boxes. Directions explain how to plant the seeds and care for the plants.

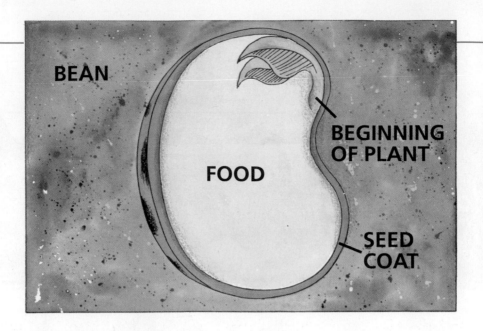

The beginning of a plant is curled up inside each seed. Food is stored inside the seed, too. The seed has a seed coat on the outside to protect it.

A seed will not sprout until certain things happen. First it must be on or in the soil. Then it needs rain to soak the seed and soften its seed coat.

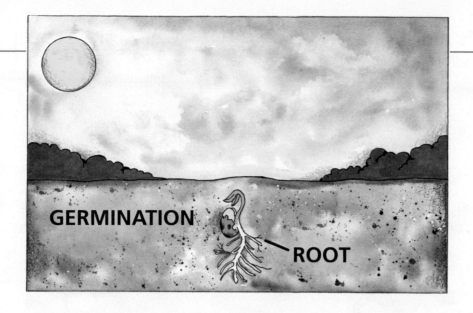

When the sun shines and warms the ground, the seed coat breaks open and the seed begins to grow. This is called germination. A root grows down into the soil. The root takes in water and minerals from the soil for food.

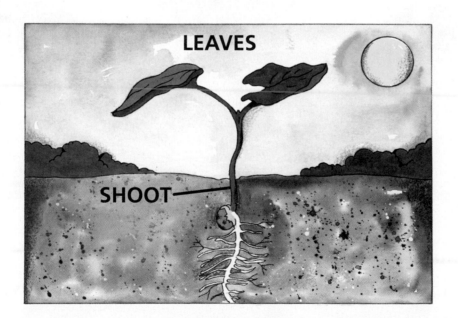

Up grows a shoot. Green leaves grow up from the shoot toward the sun. The plant grows bigger and bigger. The leaves make food for the plant from the water and minerals in the soil, the sunlight, and the air all around the plant.

Finally, the plant is full-grown. Buds on the
plant open into flowers where new seeds will grow.

Many of the foods people eat are seeds, fruits
and pods.  They are full of nutrition, vitamins and
minerals and . . . they are tasty, too!

# A "FROM SEED TO PLANT" PROJECT

**1** Find a clean glass jar. Take a piece of black construction paper and roll it up.

**2** Slide the paper into the jar. Fill the jar with water.

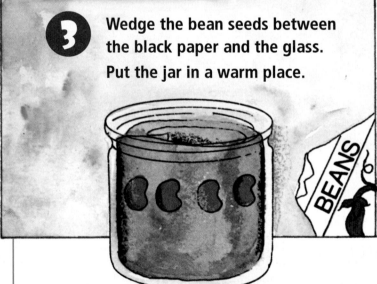

**3** Wedge the bean seeds between the black paper and the glass. Put the jar in a warm place.

BEANS

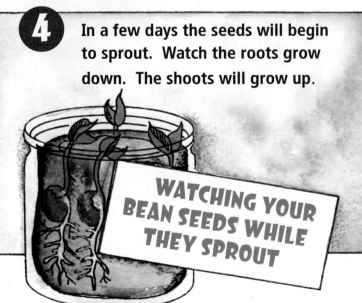

**4** In a few days the seeds will begin to sprout. Watch the roots grow down. The shoots will grow up.

WATCHING YOUR BEAN SEEDS WHILE THEY SPROUT

**ANALYZE THE TEXT**

**Cause and Effect** What causes the beans to sprout in the glass container?

362

# CARING FOR YOUR BEAN PLANTS

**5** Put dirt into a big clay pot.

**6** Carefully remove the small plants from the glass jar. Place them in the soil, covering them up to the base of their shoots.

**7** Water them . . . and watch them grow!

FROM SEED TO PLANT
BY GAIL GIBBONS

# Dig Deeper

## Use Clues to Analyze the Text

Use these pages to learn about Text and Graphic Features and Cause and Effect. Then read *From Seed to Plant* again. Use what you learn to understand it better.

## Text and Graphic Features

In *From Seed to Plant*, you read about how plants grow. The selection has text and graphic features that can help you understand more about the text. The pictures and diagrams are **graphic features** that help you better understand the topic. The labels on the diagrams are **text features** that show different parts of the diagram.

As you read, use a chart to list text and graphic features. Then list how each makes the text clear.

| Text or Graphic Feature | Page Number | Purpose |
|---|---|---|
|  |  |  |

# Cause and Effect

Sometimes one event makes another happen. For example, sunlight and water fall on a young plant. As a result, it grows. The plant getting sun and water is the **cause.** The plant growing is the **effect.** As you read, think about how one event causes another to happen as a plant grows. Think about why the events must happen in order.

# Your Turn

 **How do plants grow and change?** Share your ideas with a partner. Talk about evidence from the text and pictures in *From Seed to Plant*. Think about what the labels and pictures help you understand. Use complete sentences.

## Classroom Conversation

Now talk about these questions with the class.

1 What information is found only in the pictures?

2 How are the plants that grow in a garden different from the plants that grow in nature? Use text evidence in your answer.

3 What are some ways that animals help new plants grow?

**WRITE ABOUT READING**

**Response** Think about what a seed needs to grow. How do the soil, water, and sun work together to help the seed begin to grow? Write a few sentences to explain. Include text evidence from the selection's words and pictures in your sentences.

### Writing Tip

Make sure all the verbs in your sentences tell about the same time frame.

# INFORMATIONAL TEXT

# SUPER SOIL

☑ **GENRE**

**Informational text** gives facts about a topic. This is a science text.

☑ **TEXT FOCUS**

A **chart** is a drawing that lists information in a clear way.

Soil contains many things. When insects, leaves, and twigs die and break down in the soil, they become humus. Tiny bits of broken rock are also found in soil. Soil holds water and air, too. The amount of humus, rock, air, and water in soil differs from place to place.

If someone promised to give you good soil for growing crops, what kind of soil would you be fortunate enough to get? Soil with lots of humus is best for growing crops.

All plants need water. They take water in through roots that grow underneath the ground. They need just the right amount of water for sprouting new growth. Too little water is harmful to plants and may cause drooping leaves.

**Corn is an important crop in the United States. To grow, it needs soil with lots of humus.**

369

Deserts are places that get little rain. There is not much humus in desert soil either. Most desert plants have shallow roots. The roots spread out just below the ground to catch rain water. Cactus plants store water in their stems. A creosote bush has waxy leaves that do not lose water in the hot sun. These plants grow well in dry desert soil. Many cactus plants have beautiful flowers. After the flowers have blossomed, they produce many tiny seeds.

## Kinds of Soil

| Topsoil | Clay Soil | Sandy Soil |
|---|---|---|
| • has a lot of humus<br>• is dark in color<br>• is best for plant growth | • is made of tiny clay pieces<br>• is sticky when wet<br>• is brown, red, or yellow | • has a lot of weathered rock<br>• feels gritty<br>• is tan or light brown |

# Compare Texts

**Discuss Text and Graphic Features** With a partner, look at the text features and graphic features in *From Seed to Plant* and *Super Soil*. List the features in each selection and talk about how they are the same and different.

## TEXT TO SELF

**Talk About Gardens** What fruits and vegetables did you see in the pictures in *From Seed to Plant*? What would you like to plant if you had your own garden? Talk about it with a partner.

## TEXT TO WORLD

**Connect to Science** With a small group, research the kinds of plants that grow in your state. Make a poster to show your work and share it with the class.

**ELA** RI.2.5, RI.2.7, W.2.7

# Grammar

**More Irregular Action Verbs** The **verbs** *say, eat, give,* and *take* tell what is happening now. Do not add *-ed* to these verbs to tell what happened in the past. Instead, use *said, ate, gave,* and *took.*

| What Is Happening Now | What Happened in the Past |
|---|---|
| We say the plant names each day. | We said the plant names yesterday. |
| I eat beans this summer. | I ate beans last summer. |
| They always give vegetables to friends. | They gave vegetables to friends last night. |
| I take apples from a tree. | I took apples from a tree. |

**Try This!** **Work with a partner. Write each sentence with the correct verb. Then read each sentence aloud.**

❶ I (taked, took) a pepper to make soup.

❷ We (ate, eated) a harvest feast.

❸ She (gived, gave) me a tour of the garden.

❹ He (said, sayed) we could pick tomatoes.

When you write, make sure the verbs in your sentences all tell about the same time.

**Incorrect: past, present**

Yesterday, Kiley looked out her window.

She sees crows eating her corn.

**Correct: past, past**

Yesterday, Kiley looked out her window.
She saw crows eating her corn.

## Connect Grammar to Writing

**When you revise your research report, check all the verbs to make sure they tell about the same time.**

# Informative Writing

☑ **Elaboration** When you write a **research report,** make sure you write the information and facts in your own words.

Rosa wrote a draft of her research report. Later, she revised her draft to put everything in her own words. She also revised to include a definition for a word that might be new to her readers.

## Writing Process Checklist

**Prewrite**

**Draft**

▶ **Revise**

☑ Do the details in each paragraph connect to the main idea?

☑ Did I use facts and include definitions?

☑ Did I write what I found in my research in my own words?

**Edit**

**Publish and Share**

## Revised Draft

Giraffes are wild animals. They

live in dry, grassy parts of Africa.
Giraffes are the world's tallest
~~The giraffe is the tallest mammal~~
animal!
~~on earth.~~ They grow to about 18

feet tall. They have long necks
Two small horns grow on top of
and spots all over their bodies.∧
their heads.
Giraffes eat the leaves of

Acacia trees are trees whose
acacia trees.∧
leaves hold a lot of water.

# Giraffes

by Rosa Marquez

Giraffes are wild animals. They live in dry, grassy parts of Africa.

Giraffes are the world's tallest animal! They grow to about 18 feet tall. They have long necks and spots all over their bodies. Two small horns grow on top of their heads.

Giraffes eat the leaves of acacia trees. Acacia trees are trees whose leaves hold a lot of water. The water from these leaves helps giraffes go for a long time without drinking. You can visit giraffes in person at most zoos.

## Reading as a Writer

How did adding a definition to her writing help you understand Rosa's report? Where can you add a definition to help your readers?

I revised my report so that all my information was in my own words.

# Write a Response to Literature

**TASK** Look back at *Gloria Who Might Be My Best Friend* and *Half-Chicken*. Think about how the author of each story shows that Julian and Half-Chicken are good friends to others. Write a response to literature for your classmates. In your writing, use examples from the two stories to explain what it means to be a good friend.

**PLAN** ································································

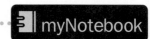 myNotebook

Use the tools in your eBook to remember details about Julian and Half-Chicken.

**Gather Information** Talk with a partner about *Gloria Who Might Be My Best Friend* and *Half-Chicken*. What makes a good friend? Are Julian and Half-Chicken good friends to others?

Then list details about each character in a chart.

- What things does Julian do that show he's a good friend?

- What things does Half-Chicken do that show he's a good friend?

| Julian | Half-Chicken |
|--------|--------------|
| • | • |
| • | • |
| • | • |

Write your draft in *my*WriteSmart.

**Write Your Response Essay** Use the information below to help you organize your essay.

> ### Main Idea Sentence
>
> Start with a strong topic sentence that explains what you feel it means to be a good friend. This sentence should be interesting and get the reader's attention.

> ### Details
>
> Tell why Julian and Half-Chicken are good friends to others. Use adjectives to help you tell what each character is like. Support your ideas with examples from each story. Use your chart to help you.

> ### Conclusion
>
> Give your paragraph a strong conclusion sentence that explains again why you feel Julian and Half-Chicken are good friends to others.

377

**my WriteSmart**

Have a partner read your draft. Talk about how you can make it better.

**Review Your Draft** Read your writing and make it better. Use the Checklist.

☑ Does my paragraph have a main idea sentence?

☑ Do all of my details support the main idea?

☑ Did I write about things that happened in the stories that show that Julian and Half-Chicken would make a good friend?

☑ Did I use adjectives to describe what each character is like?

PRESENT

**Share** Write or type a copy of your essay. Pick a way to share.

- Read your paragraph to your classmates.

- Combine your essay with others to make a class book about friendship.

Julian and Half-Chicken

# UNIT 6

# What a Surprise!

**Stream to Start**

> "" Each day holds a surprise. ""

— Henri Nouwen

## Performance Task Preview

At the end of this unit, you will think about one of the stories you have read. Then you will write your opinion of the story for others to read.

hmhfyi.com

Channel One News®

THE MYSTERIOUS TADPOLE
25TH ANNIVERSARY EDITION
NEW ILLUSTRATIONS AND TEXT BY
STEVEN KELLOGG

From **Eggs** to **Frogs**

## 🔍 LANGUAGE DETECTIVE

**Talk About Words**
**Adjectives** describe how something looks, tastes, feels, sounds, or smells. Work with a partner. Find the Vocabulary words that are adjectives. Tell what each adjective describes in the sentence.

**≡ myNotebook**

Add new words to **myWordList**. Use them in your speaking and writing.

# Vocabulary in Context

▶ **Read each Context Card.**

▶ **Use a Vocabulary word to tell about something you did.**

**1**   **ordinary**
An ostrich is not an ordinary bird. It runs quickly but cannot fly.

**2**   **control**
This rider uses reins to stay in control of the camel.

### 3. cage

If you own an iguana, you can let it out of its cage.

### 4. upset

This animal is upset because it sees danger.

### 5. sensible

These sensible hippos are smart enough to roll in cool mud on a hot day.

### 6. confused

Jack was confused. He had never seen an animal like this before!

### 7. training

The training of a ferret takes time and patience.

### 8. suspiciously

The wolf looked at the woman suspiciously. It does not trust her.

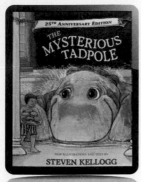

# Read and Comprehend

**Story Structure** Stories have characters, a setting, and a plot. **Characters** are people or animals in a story. The **setting** is where and when the story takes place. The **plot** is what happens in the story. A plot often has a problem that is solved at the end of the story.

Look for text evidence that tells you about the characters, the setting, and the plot. You can use a story map like this one to show the main parts of a story.

| Characters | Setting |
|:---:|:---:|
| **Plot**<br>**Problem**<br>**Solution** | |

✓ **TARGET STRATEGY**

**Infer/Predict** Use clues, or text evidence, to figure out more about story parts.

## Life Cycles

All living things change as they grow. When most living things are born, they are different than when they are grown. Think about how people change. A baby looks and acts differently than a child. A child looks and acts differently than an adult. The changes that happen as a living thing grows are called its life cycle.

You will read about how Louis's pet grows in *The Mysterious Tadpole*.

### 💬 Think | Write | Pair | Share

Think about the life cycle of a person. Write sentences that tell how you have changed since you were a baby. Discuss your sentences with a partner. Then share your sentences with the class.

## ✓ GENRE

A **fantasy** is a story that could not happen in real life. As you read, look for:

- ▸ events that could not really happen
- ▸ characters that are not found in real life

**MEET THE AUTHOR AND ILLUSTRATOR**

## Steven Kellogg

More than twenty-five years ago, Steven Kellogg first wrote and illustrated *The Mysterious Tadpole.* Then, for the book's big anniversary, he published a new version with different illustrations and words. The new version is the one you are about to read.

# THE MYSTERIOUS TADPOLE

written and illustrated by
**Steven Kellogg**

**ESSENTIAL QUESTION**

How do some animals
change as they grow?

"Greetings, nephew!" cried Louis's uncle McAllister. "I've brought a wee bit of Scotland for your birthday."

"Thanks!" said Louis. "Look, Mom and Dad. It's a TADPOLE!"

Louis named him Alphonse and promised to take very good care of him.

Louis took Alphonse to school for show-and-tell.

"Class, here we have a splendid example of a tadpole," exclaimed Ms. Shelbert. "Let's ask Louis to bring it back every week so we can watch it become a frog."

Ms. Shelbert was amazed to see how quickly Alphonse grew.

"Maybe it's because he only eats cheeseburgers," said Louis.

When Alphonse became too big for his jar, Louis moved him to the kitchen sink. "He's the perfect pet!" said Louis.

Louis and Alphonse loved to play games.

"Be careful, Louis," said his mother. "The living room is not a soccer field. Something is going to get broken!"

And she was right. That same day the soccer ball slammed into Aunt Tabitha's antique lamp.

"This tadpole is out of control," said Louis's mother. "Something must be done."

"It won't happen again," promised Louis. "I'll take Alphonse to obedience school."

The only animals at the obedience school were dogs.

Some of their owners stared at Alphonse suspiciously.

"Pretend you're a dog," whispered Louis.

Alphonse tried to bark, but it sounded like a burp.

"Hold on a minute," said the trainer. "What kind of dog is this?"

"He's a hairless spotted water spaniel from Scotland," explained Louis.

Alphonse quickly learned to SIT, STAY, and RETRIEVE. He graduated at the top of his class.

"My parents will be very pleased," said Louis.

But Louis's parents were not pleased when Alphonse
outgrew the sink and had to be moved to the bathtub.

"This shower is too crowded," complained Louis's father.

"This bathroom is a mess," moaned Louis's mother.

At least Louis's classmates enjoyed Alphonse, who was still making weekly visits.

"Wow! Show-and-tell is more fun than recess!" they yelled.

But one day Ms. Shelbert decided that Alphonse was not turning into an ordinary frog. She asked Louis to stop bringing him to school.

**ANALYZE THE TEXT**

**Conclusions** How do the illustrations give you clues that Alphonse is not a tadpole?

By the time summer vacation arrived, Alphonse had outgrown the bathtub.

"We could buy the parking lot next door and build him a swimming pool," suggested Louis.

"Be sensible," declared Louis's parents. "Swimming pools are expensive. We're sorry, Louis, but this situation has become impossible. Tomorrow you will have to take your tadpole to the zoo."

"But I can't put my friend in a cage!" cried Louis.

That night Louis was very sad—until he remembered that the gym in the nearby high school had a swimming pool.

Louis hid Alphonse under a carpet and smuggled him inside.

"Nobody uses this place during the summer," whispered Louis. "You'll be safe here."

After making sure that Alphonse felt at home, Louis said good-bye. "I'll be back tomorrow with a big pile of cheeseburgers," he promised.

Louis came every afternoon to play with Alphonse.
In the mornings he earned the money for the
cheeseburgers by delivering newspapers.

The training continued as well.

Louis would say, "Alphonse, RETRIEVE!"

And Alphonse would succeed every time.

As summer vacation passed, Louis became more
and more worried about what would happen to
Alphonse when the high school kids returned.

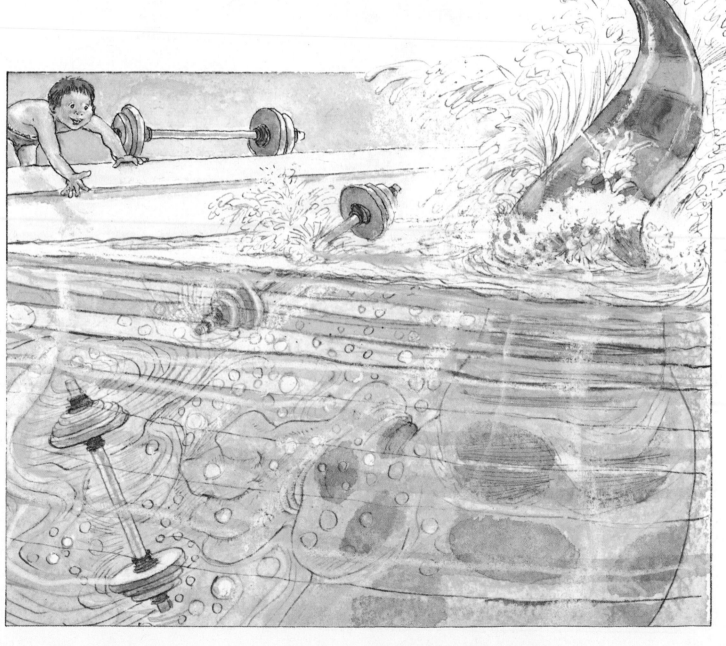

After his first day of classes Louis ran to the high school, and found the gym bustling with activity. The swim team was heading for the pool.

"STOP!" cried Louis.

"On your mark!" bellowed the coach. "Get set!"

"Excuse me, sir," said Louis.

"GO!" roared the coach.

Alphonse rose to the surface to welcome the swimmers.

"It's a submarine from another planet!" shrieked the coach.

"Call the police! Call the Navy!"

"No, it's only a tadpole," said Louis. "He's my pet."

The coach was upset and confused.

"You have until tomorrow," he cried, "to get that creature out of the pool!"

Louis telephoned his friend Ms. Seevers, the librarian, and asked for her help.

"I'll be right there!" she said.

Ms. Seevers rushed to meet Louis at the high school. When she saw Alphonse, she was so startled that she dropped her purse into the water.

"RETRIEVE!" said Louis. And Alphonse did.

"Where did this astounding animal come from?" cried Ms. Seevers.

"He was a birthday gift from my uncle," Louis replied.

Ms. Seevers telephoned Uncle McAllister.

"Oh, the wee tadpole?" he said. "Why, he came from the lake nearby. It's the one folks call Loch Ness."

"Brace yourself, Louis!" Ms. Seevers said. "I believe your uncle found the Loch Ness monster!"

"I don't care!" cried Louis. "Alphonse is my friend and I love him." He pleaded with Ms. Seevers to help him raise enough money to buy the parking lot so he could build a big swimming pool for Alphonse.

Suddenly Ms. Seevers had an idea. "Long ago a pirate ship sank in the harbor," she said. "No one has ever been able to find it—or its treasure chest. But perhaps we can!"

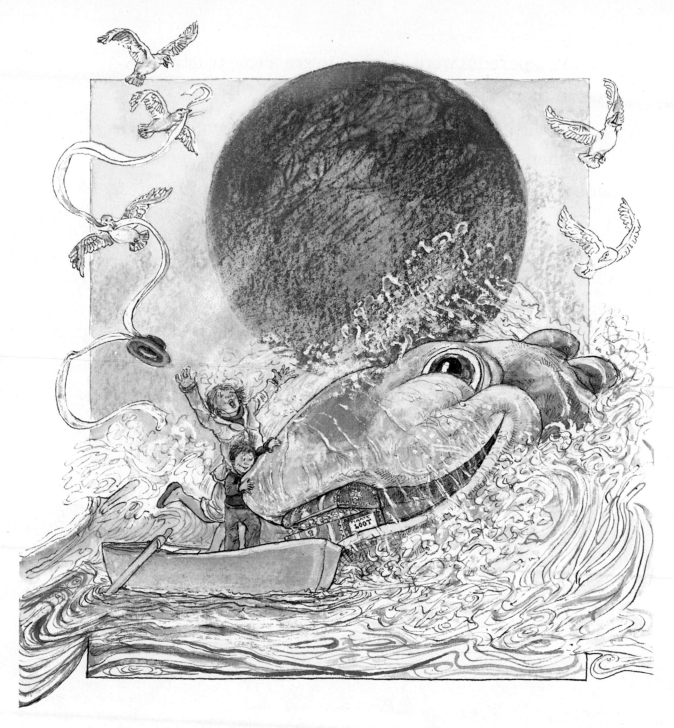

The next morning they drove to the harbor and rented a boat.

"This is a treasure chest," cried Louis. "RETRIEVE!"

Alphonse disappeared under the water and returned with the chest! It was filled with gold and jewels.

"Let's buy the parking lot and get to work!" cried Ms. Seevers.

Louis's parents were shocked to see a construction
crew in the parking lot.

"Louis!" they cried. "What in the world is going on here?"

"Alphonse found a pirate treasure ship," explained
Louis. "And we used part of our gold to buy you this present."

Louis's parents were shocked once again. "Tickets for a vacation cruise to Hawaii!" they gasped.

"And," said Louis, "you don't have to worry about us, because Granny has agreed to baby-sit." They hugged Louis. They kissed Alphonse.

"How soon can we leave?" they cried.

"Immediately," said Louis.

By the time Louis's parents returned, the swimming pool was being enjoyed by everyone in the city.

A week later Louis said, "Alphonse, tomorrow is my birthday, which means that you've been my best friend for a whole year."

The next day Uncle McAllister arrived for the party.

"Greetings, Louis my lad!" he exclaimed. "I've come with a curious stone from the hills of Scotland. Happy Birthday!"

"Wow! Thanks!" said Louis. Suddenly the stone began to tremble and crack . . .

---

**ANALYZE THE TEXT**

**Story Structure** How is the problem with Alphonse solved? What problem might the new birthday gift cause?

# Dig Deeper

## Use Clues to Analyze the Text

Use these pages to learn about Story Structure and Conclusions. Then read *The Mysterious Tadpole* again. Use what you learn to understand it better.

## Story Structure

The *Mysterious Tadpole* is about a boy who gets an unusual pet. The characters, the setting, and the plot of the story make up the **story structure**. The beginning of a story usually tells the characters, setting, and what problem the characters have. The end of the story tells how the problem is solved.

Use a story map to record text evidence that will help you describe the story structure.

| Characters | Setting |
|:---:|:---:|
| **Plot**<br>**Problem**<br>**Solution** | |

# Conclusions

Authors do not always tell readers everything they want them to know. Readers must ask and answer questions to draw **conclusions** about what the author does not say. Text evidence, such as clues in the words and pictures, can help you draw conclusions. For example, you might ask yourself where the story takes place. You can look at the pictures in the story to figure it out when the author doesn't tell you.

# Your Turn

 **Turn and Talk**

**How do some animals change as they grow?** Share your ideas with a partner. Use text evidence from *The Mysterious Tadpole* in your discussion. Take turns speaking.

## 💬 Classroom Conversation

Now talk about these questions with the class.

**1** What will happen after the stone begins to crumble? Why do you think so?

**2** How do the pictures help you understand more about the characters, the setting, and the plot? Give an example for each.

**3** Do you think Uncle McAllister knew that Alphonse was not a tadpole? Why or why not?

### WRITE ABOUT READING

**Response** In the beginning of *The Mysterious Tadpole*, the characters think that Alphonse is a tadpole. Think about how tadpoles grow into frogs. Then write text evidence from the words and pictures in the story to prove that Alphonse is not a tadpole.

### Writing Tip

Remember that irregular action verbs do not have *-ed* added to them to tell what happened in the past.

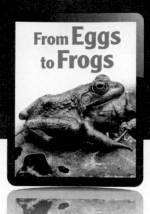
# From Eggs to Frogs

## From Egg to Tadpole

Many frogs start life as an egg that hatches in an ordinary pond. The young are called tadpoles. You may look at them suspiciously and feel confused. Why? Tadpoles look like tiny fish, not frogs.

### Life Cycle of a Frog

 A frog lays lots of eggs.

 Tadpoles hatch from the eggs.

## From Tadpole to Frog

A tadpole has a tail but no legs. It uses its tail to stay in control as it swims. A tadpole lives underwater and breathes through gills. As a tadpole grows, it begins to look like a frog. A frog has legs and lungs but no tail. A frog lives out of water part of the time.

Some animals care for their young and teach them how to find food. A tadpole gets no training from its parents. It is able to find its own food.

③ The tadpole grows legs. Lungs develop. The tail shrinks.

④ The tadpole has become a frog.

## Frogs as Pets

It is a good idea to keep your frog in a fish tank, not a cage. Put water in the tank and rocks for the frog to climb on. Sensible owners handle their frogs gently so the frogs do not become upset. They give their frogs water, plants, and the good food they need.

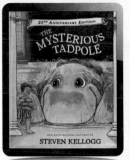

# Compare Texts

**Examine Author's Purpose** What was the author's purpose for writing *The Mysterious Tadpole*? What was the author's purpose for writing *From Eggs to Frogs*? Write a few sentences to explain how the authors' reasons for writing were different.

## TEXT TO SELF

**Tell About a Gift** How would you feel if you received Louis's birthday gift? Why? Share your feelings with a partner.

## TEXT TO WORLD

**Connect to Science** Think about real tadpoles and how they change into frogs. With a partner, choose another animal to research. Write a few sentences about how the animal changes as it grows. Then draw a diagram. Present the diagram to the class to explain the changes.

ELA RL.2.1, RI.2.1, RI.2.6, W.2.7, SL.2.5

# Grammar

**Digital Resources**

► Multimedia Grammar Glossary

► GrammarSnap Video

**Contractions** A **contraction** is a short way of writing two words. An **apostrophe** (') shows where letters were left out.

| Whole Words | Contractions |
|---|---|
| do not | don't |
| that is | that's |
| is not | isn't |
| I am | I'm |
| I will | I'll |
| we are | we're |
| it is | it's |

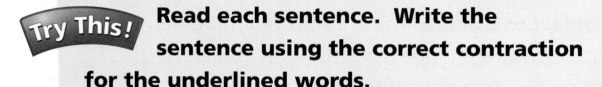

**Try This!** **Read each sentence. Write the sentence using the correct contraction for the underlined words.**

❶ I <u>do</u> <u>not</u> think that is a frog!

❷ <u>I</u> <u>am</u> sure <u>it</u> <u>is</u> a lake monster.

❸ <u>We</u> <u>are</u> going to the library.

When you use contractions in your writing, be sure to spell them correctly. Remember to put the apostrophe (') in the right place.

| Wrong | Correct |
|---|---|
| That is'nt a tadpole. | That isn't a tadpole. |
| Thats' a dinosaur! | That's a dinosaur! |

## Connect Grammar to Writing

**When you edit your poem, make sure that contractions are spelled correctly and apostrophes are in the right place.**

# Opinion Writing

✓ **Elaboration**  When you write a poem, use sense words and details to make your feelings or opinion clear.

Luke drafted a poem in response to *The Mysterious Tadpole*.  Later, he revised his writing to include more sense words and details.

## Writing Checklist

✓ **Organization**
Did I write my poem with lines that rhyme?

✓ **Evidence**
Did I use powerful language to show my opinion?

✓ **Elaboration**
Did I use sense words and details?

✓ **Conventions**
Do my sentences make sense in the poem?

### Revised Draft

                    funny
Alphonse is a pet.
                ∧

He is very wild and wet.
                loud
Alphonse has a laugh and likes
                ∧

to play.

He gets bigger every day.

He should probably live in a zoo.
        I had a giant Alphonse, too!
I wish ~~Alphonse could live~~
        ∧

~~with me!~~

# A Funny Pet

by Luke Beem

Alphonse is a funny pet.
He is very wild and wet.
Alphonse has a loud laugh and likes to play.
He gets bigger every day.
He should probably live in a zoo.
I wish I had a giant Alphonse, too!

## Reading as a Writer

How do the sense words and details that Luke added make his poem more interesting? What words and details can you add to your own poem?

I added sense words and details to make my poem more interesting.

417

La Brea Tar Pits

**Q LANGUAGE DETECTIVE**

**Talk About Words**
**Verbs** are words that name actions. Work with a partner. Find the Vocabulary words that are verbs. What are your clues? Use the verbs in new sentences.

# Vocabulary in Context

▶ Read each **Context Card**.

▶ Make up a new sentence that uses a Vocabulary word.

**1** **exact**

The map showed the exact place to dig for old bones.

**2** **discovered**

This old shark's tooth was discovered on a beach. It was found by a scientist.

### 3 remove

This scientist uses a brush to gently remove, or take away, sand.

### 4 growled

The dog growled and barked as it dug up the old bone.

### 5 amazed

The girl was amazed at the size of the dinosaur teeth in the museum.

### 6 explained

The man explained, or told, about the dinosaur.

### 7 guard

A guard makes sure no one touches anything in the museum.

### 8 souvenirs

He bought souvenirs to remember his day at the museum.

# Read and Comprehend

**TARGET SKILL**

**Fact and Opinion** A **fact** is something that can be proved to be true or false. An **opinion** is what someone believes or feels. Authors often use facts to back up, or support, their opinions.

You can keep track of facts and opinions in a chart like this one.

| Fact | Opinion |
|------|---------|
|      |         |

**TARGET STRATEGY**

**Question** Ask questions about what you are reading. Look for text evidence to answer your questions.

**ELA** RI.2.1, RI.2.8, SL.2.1a, SL.2.3

## Fossils

Sometimes parts of animals or plants that lived long ago can be found today. These are called fossils. An animal bone is an example of a fossil. Fossils can be found all over the world. Scientists look for fossils to help them learn about the past. Some fossils are on display at museums.

You will read about a girl and her dog who discovered fossils in *The Dog That Dug for Dinosaurs.*

### 💬 Talk About It

Have you or anyone you know ever seen a fossil? What kind of fossil was it, and where was it seen? Discuss with your class. Ask questions if you don't understand something.

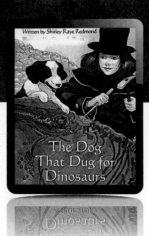

The Dog That Dug for Dinosaurs

**☑ GENRE**

A **biography** tells about events in a person's life. As you read, look for:

▸ information about why a person is important

▸ events in time order

**MEET THE AUTHOR**

# Shirley Raye Redmond

At her home in New Mexico, Shirley Raye Redmond begins her day by waking up early and watching the many birds that come to the feeders in her yard. Then she's ready to sit down and start writing.

**MEET THE ILLUSTRATOR**

# Stacey Schuett

Even as a child, Stacey Schuett wanted to be an artist or a writer. "I was a dreamy kind of little kid who loved to make stuff up," she says. She has illustrated many books, including ones about pirates and trees.

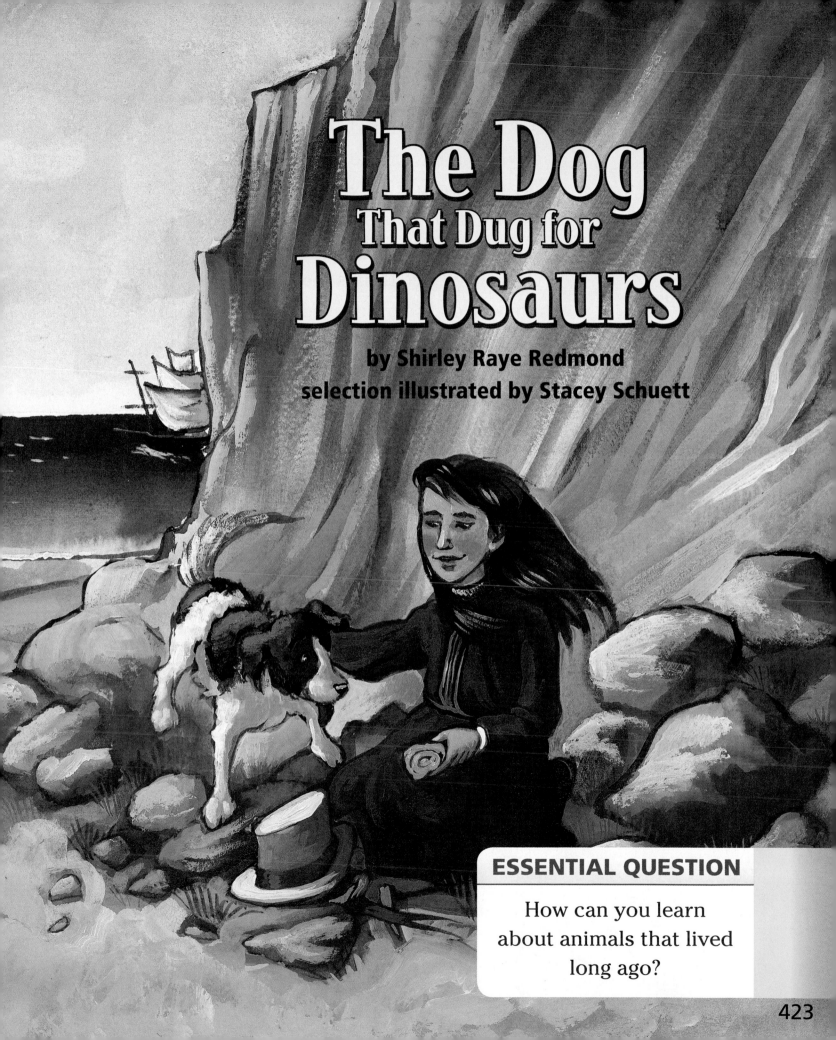

# The Dog
## That Dug for
# Dinosaurs

**by Shirley Raye Redmond**

**selection illustrated by Stacey Schuett**

**ESSENTIAL QUESTION**

How can you learn
about animals that lived
long ago?

A LONG, LONG TIME AGO, there was a little dog named Tray. He was black-and-white all over. He had friendly brown eyes and a very wiggly tail. Tray lived in England. Tray was a real dog, and this is an honestly true story about him.

Tray loved two things most in the whole world. First, he loved Mary Anning. She was twelve years old and lived with her family in a small cottage near the beach in Lyme Regis. Secondly, Tray loved going with Mary to dig for fossils.

So, what are fossils anyway? They are the remains of animals and plants that died a long time ago. When a leaf or bone gets pressed between layers of sea mud, it leaves an imprint. After many, many years, the mud hardens to rock.

Tray and Mary knew that they would find the very best fossils high up on the cliffs around the beach. They climbed up there every day.

Tray sniffed the rocks. *Sniff, sniff.* He pawed the dirt. *Scratch, scratch.* Mary used a small hammer and chisel. *Tap, tap, tap.*

With these tools, Mary carefully cut fossils out of the cliff, just as her father had shown her. Tray watched as she placed the fossils in her basket. Most of them looked like seashells. Mary and Tray sold them as souvenirs to the tourists that came by stagecoach to swim at the beach near their home.

One day Tray and Mary discovered some
very large bones sticking out of the rocks.  They were
*huge*!

Tray growled and tried to dig the bones out.

Mary used her hands to brush away the
loose dirt.

"Tray, we've discovered a monster!" she declared.

The bones were much too big for Tray and Mary to
remove by themselves.

"I'll go for help," Mary said. "You stay here, Tray."

Tray barked loudly and sat down in front of the
bones.  He was a very good guard dog.

Mary ran all the way back to town and asked some grown-ups to help her. "Tray and I have found something really special in the cliff," she told them. "Just wait and see!"

When the men saw the giant rib bones in the side of the cliff, they were amazed. "What a beast!" they cried.

"Look at those sharp teeth!"

"Is it a crocodile?" one man asked. "Or a stubby whale?"

"We don't know what it is," Mary admitted. "But we know it's something special, don't we, Tray?"

Tray yipped and wagged his tail.

A rich man who lived nearby heard about the sea monster. He hurried to see it for himself.

"I'll buy it!" he cried. "I will give it to the British Museum in London."

"Do you know what it is?" Mary asked.

"It is called an ichthyosaur (ICK-thee-uh-soar)," the man told her.

"That means 'fish lizard,'" he explained. "It's like a dinosaur with fins."

**ANALYZE THE TEXT**

**Fact and Opinion** What is Mary's opinion about what she finds? What facts do you learn about it?

429

The amazing news spread about the gigantic fish lizard and the dog and little girl who had found it.

Soon many strangers came to Lyme Regis where Mary and Tray lived. They all wanted to hunt for fossils too. The men wore tall top hats. The women wore frilly bonnets. They carried pretty umbrellas called parasols.

Mary shook her head and smiled. She rubbed Tray's soft ears. They watched the strangers together.

"They don't have the right tools," Mary whispered. "They are wearing the wrong kinds of shoes. Aren't they silly, Tray?"

Tray yipped and chased his tail.

Curious scientists visited Lyme Regis too.
One man came from the university in Oxford.
His name was William Buckland. He went to the
old carpenter's shop where Mary and Tray sold their
fossils.

"Can you show me where you found your
ichthyosaur, young lady?" he asked politely. "Do you
think you could find the exact spot again?"

"Tray can find it," Mary boasted.

Together Mary and Mr. Buckland followed the little dog across the beach and up to the cliffs.

Tray sniffed the rocks. *Sniff, sniff.*

He pawed the dirt. *Scratch, scratch.*

Suddenly he yipped. Then he sat down. Mary pointed. It was the exact place where she had discovered the strange fish lizard!

"What an intelligent dog!" Mr. Buckland declared.

Tray wagged his tail.

Tray and Mary continued to dig for fossils. They were very careful. Mary watched for falling rocks, like her dad told her. Tray looked out for storms and high tides. Then one day they discovered another giant creature.

"Look, Tray!" Mary cried. "Is it a sea dragon?"

Tray sniffed the skeleton and snapped at it with his teeth. The creature had a long, long neck. Its backbone was like a humped turtle shell. Instead of feet and legs, it had four large paddles.

But it wasn't a sea dragon.

Mr. Buckland called it a plesiosaur (PLEE-zee-uh-soar).

One day, Tray and Mary found a fossil that no one in England had ever found before. This one had huge bony wings like a bat and a long sharp jaw.

Tray growled.

"It looks like a gigantic flying lizard!" Mary declared.

The scientists thought so too, and that's why they named it a pterodactyl (TAIR-uh-DACK-til).

That means "lizard with wings."

Over the years, Tray, Mary, and Mr. Buckland became good friends.

They showed him where to find the best fossils in Lyme Regis.

Mr. Buckland brought books about dinosaurs for Mary. He brought beef bones for Tray. Mary, with Tray on her lap, studied her books every day.

When Tray's whiskers turned gray and Mary was all grown up, they still collected fossils and sold them in the old carpenter's shop. There were boxes and baskets filled with fossils on the floor and on the shelves. Some of the fossil creatures were so big they couldn't fit through the door!

Sometimes children and tourists stopped in to buy fossils of ancient sand dollars or tiny fish and curly shells. Many scientists came to the shop to buy fossils too. They brought carts and wagons to haul away the really large ones.

Tray and Mary Anning became very famous. Today, if you go to the Natural History Museum in London, you can see the large fossils they discovered together.

You can also see a famous painting of Mary holding her fossil basket, and Tray, the dog that dug for dinosaurs.

**ANALYZE THE TEXT**

**Author's Purpose** What is the author's purpose for writing about Mary and Tray?

# Dig Deeper

## Use Clues to Analyze the Text

Use these pages to learn about Fact and Opinion and Author's Purpose. Then read *The Dog That Dug for Dinosaurs* again. Use what you learn to understand it better.

## Fact and Opinion

In *The Dog That Dug for Dinosaurs*, you read facts about real events. A **fact** is something that can be proved to be true. An **opinion** is what someone believes or feels.

As you reread, look for reasons that support facts and opinions. For example, the author writes that Mary Anning became famous. She supports that by writing that Mary's picture is in a museum. Use a chart like this one to list facts and opinions that the author gives support for.

| Fact | Opinion |
|------|---------|
|      |         |

# Author's Purpose

The reason why an author writes something is called the **author's purpose**. The author's purpose may be to give information or to make a reader laugh. The purpose may also be to make a reader believe something or to answer a question. Think about why the author wrote *The Dog That Dug for Dinosaurs*.

# Your Turn

 **Turn and Talk**

**How can you learn about animals that lived long ago?** Talk about your ideas with a partner. Be sure to use text evidence from *The Dog That Dug for Dinosaurs* to explain your thoughts. Ask your partner to explain more if you don't understand his or her ideas.

## Classroom Conversation

Now talk about these questions with the class.

1. Why did scientists like William Buckland come to see the fossils?

2. Why did Mary think that she found a monster when she found her first dinosaur?

3. What opinions did different people have about the fossils that Mary and Tray found?

**WRITE ABOUT READING** ·································

**Response** How did finding the fossils change Mary's life? Write a paragraph to explain your answer using facts and text evidence.

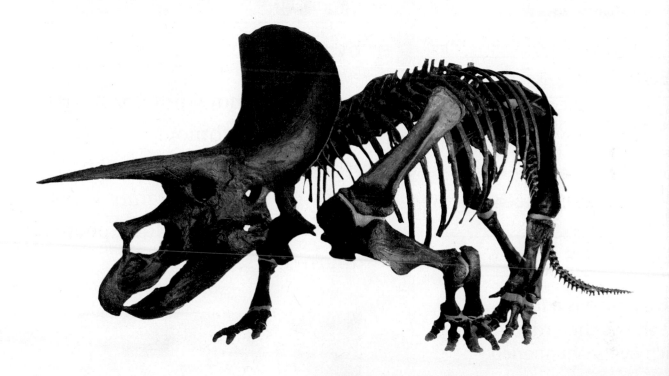

### Writing Tip

Remember to end your paragraph with a closing sentence. A closing sentence gives your writing a clear ending.

# INFORMATIONAL TEXT

La Brea
Tar Pits

## ✓ GENRE

**Informational text** gives facts about a topic. This is a newspaper article.

## ✓ TEXT FOCUS

A **time line** is a line that shows the order in which events happened.

# DAILY NEWS

FRIDAY, JANUARY 18

# La Brea Tar Pits

by Ciara McLaughlin

Did you know that Los Angeles, California, is famous for its tar pits? They are the La Brea Tar Pits, to be exact. Scientists remove lots of fossils from them. Many people are amazed to see the fossils.

**La Brea is one of the best places in the world to find fossils.**

**Life-size statues of mammoths at the La Brea Tar Pits**

Scientists have explained that Los Angeles was once cooler and wetter than it is today. They know this because fossils of plants and animals that lived only in cool, wet places have been discovered there. These plants and animals lived a very long time ago. The animals included big cats with huge teeth. Imagine how they growled! Other animals had to be on guard if they did not want to be eaten.

**A saber-toothed cat skull**

At times, wolves chased mammoths into tar pits. Then the sticky tar trapped them all. The trapped animals died. Over time, they became fossils.

The tar still traps living things. In time, they may become fossils. People may find them and keep them as souvenirs.

Scientists searching for fossils at the La Brea Tar Pits

## La Brea Time Line

| More than 100,000 years ago | About 100,000 years ago | About 40,000 years ago | Today |
|---|---|---|---|
| Area covered by water | Water goes down, and land appears | First plants and animals trapped | Surrounded by a busy city |

# Compare Texts

**Think About Fossils** Reread page 446. Talk to a partner about how animals become fossils. Then discuss how that helps you understand how animals became fossils in *The Dog That Dug for Dinosaurs.*

**Tell About a Discovery** You read about how finding dinosaur bones changed Mary's life. How would finding a fossil change your life?

**Connect to Social Studies** Why is Mary Anning an important person? Work with a partner to write about how her discoveries might have helped people.

# Grammar

**What Is an Adverb?** An **adverb** is a word that describes a **verb.** An adverb can tell how something happens. It can also tell when something happens.

| Adverbs That Tell How | Adverbs That Tell When |
| --- | --- |
| Tray and I slowly dug in the dirt. | Before the trip, I got some tools. |
| We pulled out the fossil gently. | Next, I put on some gloves. |

 **Work with a partner. Choose the word that best completes each sentence. Then read the sentence aloud.**

❶ (Early, After) lunch, I went to the museum.

❷ My dog barked (loudly, loud) to warn of danger.

❸ The man worked (careful, carefully) to uncover the fossil.

Sometimes you may write two sentences with adverbs that tell about the same verb. Join the sentences, using *and* between the two adverbs. This will make your writing smoother.

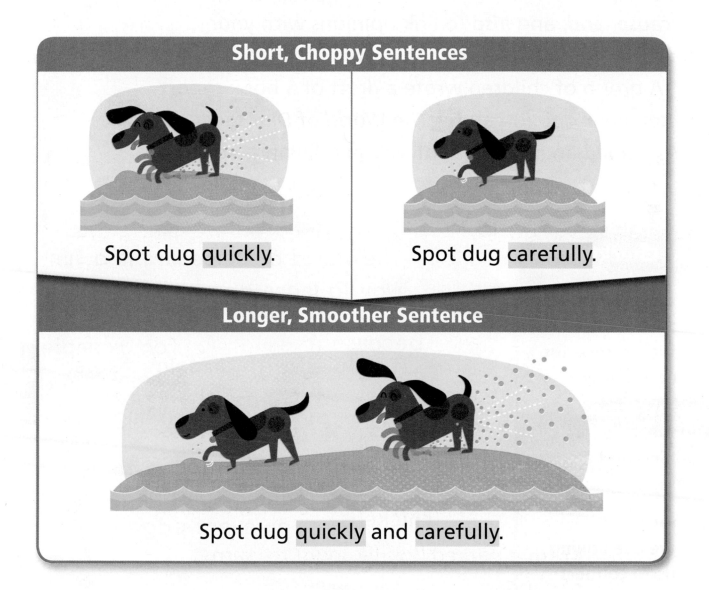

**Short, Choppy Sentences**

Spot dug quickly.

Spot dug carefully.

**Longer, Smoother Sentence**

Spot dug quickly and carefully.

## Connect Grammar to Writing

When you revise your opinion paragraph, combine sentences with adverbs that tell about the same verb.

# Opinion Writing

✓ **Organization** When you write a book report, write your opinion of the book in the **opening sentence.** Then explain your reasons. Use words such as *because*, *and*, and *also* to link opinions with your reasons. Write a **closing sentence** at the end.

A group of children wrote a draft of a book report to tell their opinion about *The World of Dinosaurs*. Later, they added an opening sentence and linking words.

## Writing Checklist

✓ **Purpose**
Did we express our opinion clearly?

✓ **Organization**
Did we write an opening and a closing sentence?

✓ **Evidence**
Did we use linking words to connect ideas?

✓ **Conventions**
Did we use resources to check our spelling?

### Revised Draft

The World of Dinosaurs is a fun way to learn about dinosaurs. The book is exciting to read.
because it
For example,
~~It~~ is filled with amazing facts.
and
not all dinosaurs were huge,

some were even smaller than
Also, there are exciting pictures
chickens. on every page.

# The World of Dinosaurs

by Ann Li, Omar Jones, and Meg Smith

*The World of Dinosaurs* is a fun way to learn about dinosaurs. The book is exciting to read because it is filled with amazing facts. For example, not all dinosaurs were huge, and some were even smaller than chickens. Also, there are exciting pictures on every page. Some show dinosaurs fighting. Others show giant skeletons that look very scary. Anyone who likes dinosaurs will enjoy reading this book.

## Reading as a Writer

How does the order of the sentences help the reader understand the opinion? How can you put your sentences in an order that makes your opinion clear?

We added connecting words to help support our opinion.

Yeh-Shen
by Gina Sabella
illustrated by Jill Dubin

Cinderella

## 🔍 LANGUAGE DETECTIVE

**Talk About Words**
Work with a partner.
Choose one of the
Context Cards. Add
words to the sentence
to explain more details
about the photo.

# Vocabulary in Context

▶ **Study each Context Card.**

▶ **Talk about a picture. Use a different Vocabulary word from the one on the card.**

**1** **task**
My grandfather gave me a
task to do. I helped him
decorate for the party.

**2** **glimmering**
The divers saw something
flash in the water. It was a
group of glimmering fish.

### 3. served

I think pizza tastes best when it is **served** fresh and hot right out of the oven!

### 4. content

The girls were **content** to play outside. It was fine with them not to watch TV.

### 5. worn

The teddy bear looks **worn**. It must be very old.

### 6. overjoyed

The children were **overjoyed** to see each other. They smiled and laughed.

### 7. concealed

A smaller doll is **concealed** inside the larger doll.

### 8. valuable

The ring is **valuable** to my mother. She has had it for many years.

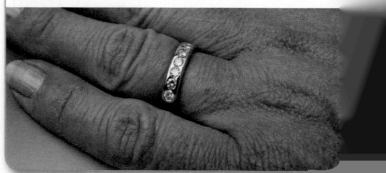

# Read and Comprehend

**TARGET SKILL**

**Sequence of Events** An author of a story often tells story events in the order that they happen. The order in which events happen is called the **sequence of events.** Thinking about the story events can help you understand the **author's message,** or what you can learn from the story. Put events in order in a chart like this one.

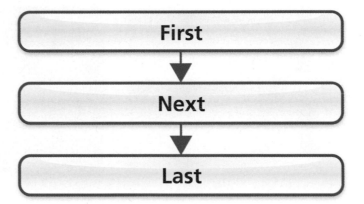

First

↓

Next

↓

Last

**TARGET STRATEGY**

**Analyze/Evaluate** To **analyze** as you read, think about the author's words and story events. Then **evaluate,** or decide, how the words and events help you know what is important in the story.

 ELA RL.2.2, SL.2.1a, SL.2.1b

## Traditional Stories

People have been telling traditional stories for many years. One kind of traditional story is a **fairy tale.** Fairy tales tell about events that could not happen in real life. The story often teaches a lesson. Fairy tales usually have a happy ending. You will read a fairy tale about a young girl in *Yeh-Shen.*

**Think | Pair | Share**

Think about fairy tales you have heard before. Discuss your favorite one and its lesson with a partner. Share your ideas with classmates.

▶ Take turns speaking.
▶ Listen carefully to others.
▶ Add to your classmates' ideas.

# ANCHOR TEXT

Yeh-Shen
by Gina Sabella
illustrated by Jill Dubin

## ✓ GENRE

A **fairy tale** is a make-believe story that has been told for many years. Look for:

▶ characters who would not exist in real life
▶ a happy ending

### MEET THE ILLUSTRATOR
# Jill Dubin

Jill Dubin always loved art, even as a child. She and her sister used to spend hours making dolls out of paper.

Ms. Dubin used paper to make the pictures for *Yeh-Shen*. First, she sketched each picture. Next, she picked pieces of paper with different colors and patterns. She cut out pieces of the paper and placed them onto the sketches. The backgrounds and the characters' clothes are all different pieces of paper glued together!

ELA RL.2.2, RL.2.10

# Yeh-Shen

by Gina Sabella    illustrated by Jill Dubin

**ESSENTIAL QUESTION**

What can you learn from reading a fairy tale?

Yeh-Shen was a girl who grew up in China a long, long time ago. Her mother and father had died, so she lived with her mean stepmother, Jin, and her stepsister, Jun-li. They lived in a cave.

Every time Jin looked at Yeh-Shen, she became angry. Yeh-Shen was gentler and kinder than Jin's own daughter, Jun-li. Yeh-Shen was also a hard worker. Jun-li was spoiled and lazy.

Jin gave Yeh-Shen only rags to wear. She gave her long lists of chores to do. When Yeh-Shen finished one task, Jin added three more to the list.

Yeh-Shen was always busy working. She did not have a chance to make many friends, but she did have one very special friend. This friend had golden eyes, glimmering scales, and a big beautiful tail. It was a fish that lived in the pond. Every day Yeh-Shen stopped by the pond and shared some crumbs with the fish. Every day the fish popped up to greet its friend.

Yeh-Shen's stepmother saw this and became furious. She didn't want Yeh-Shen to have any friends, not even a fish! One day, Jin caught the fish and cooked it for dinner.

Yeh-Shen cried when she saw her friend served for dinner. She ran out of the cave and sat by the pond.

"What's the matter?" an old man asked her.

Yeh-Shen told him about her friend, the fish. Then she told him what her stepmother had done.

"Listen carefully to me," the old man said. "The bones of that fish hold special powers. Take the bones and bury them in four pots. Put one pot at each corner of your bed. Whenever you need help, tell the bones what you need. They will make your every wish come true."

Yeh-Shen followed the old man's directions. When she got back to the cave, she buried the bones in four pots. Then she put the pots by the corners of her bed. She did not have anything to ask for yet, but she felt content knowing that her friend was close by.

A few weeks later, the spring festival arrived. At the festival, young men and women could meet. They hoped to fall in love and marry.

Jin didn't want to ruin Jun-li's chances of finding a husband, so she ordered Yeh-Shen to stay home and clean. Then she and Jun-li went to the festival.

**ANALYZE THE TEXT**

**Compare and Contrast** Does the stepmother treat Jun-li and Yeh-Shen in the same way? Explain your answer using text evidence.

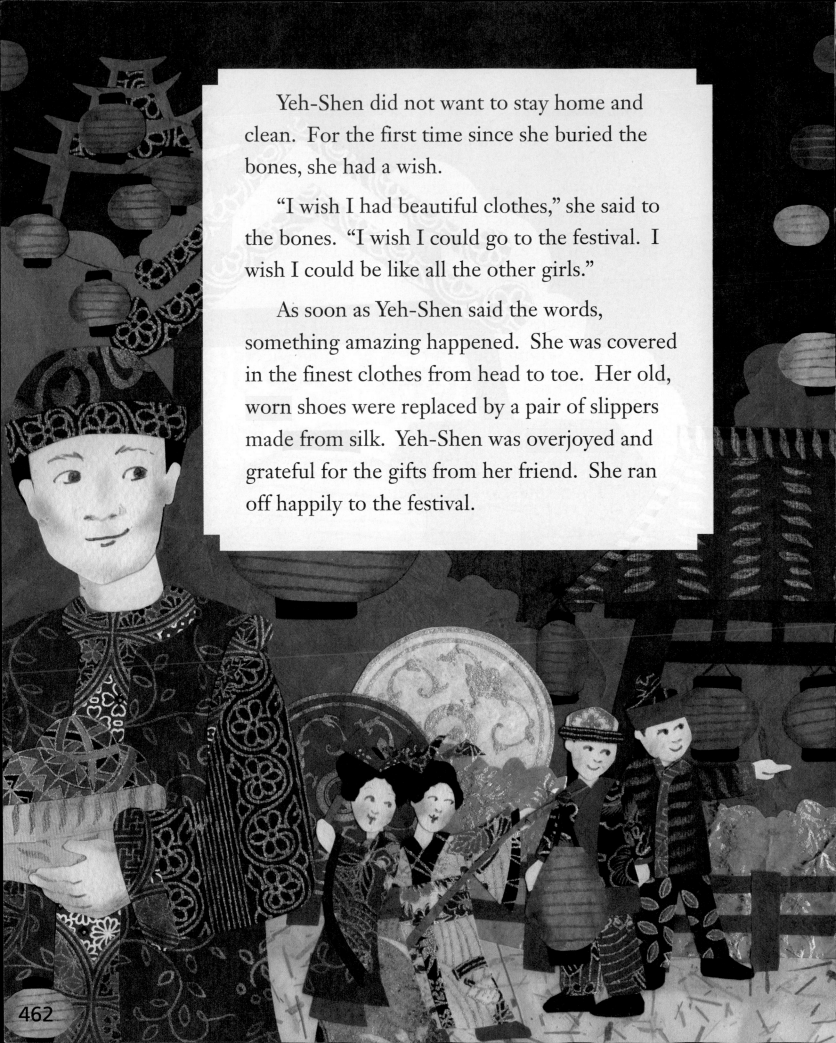

Yeh-Shen did not want to stay home and clean. For the first time since she buried the bones, she had a wish.

"I wish I had beautiful clothes," she said to the bones. "I wish I could go to the festival. I wish I could be like all the other girls."

As soon as Yeh-Shen said the words, something amazing happened. She was covered in the finest clothes from head to toe. Her old, worn shoes were replaced by a pair of slippers made from silk. Yeh-Shen was overjoyed and grateful for the gifts from her friend. She ran off happily to the festival.

Everyone at the festival stopped to stare at Yeh-Shen when she walked in. Who was this beautiful girl in the magnificent clothes?

Yeh-Shen had a wonderful time at the festival, but she was worried that her stepmother would notice her. She decided to hurry home, but she ran so fast that one of her silk slippers fell off. It lay in the middle of the road. It was the only sign that Yeh-Shen had visited the festival.

At home, Yeh-Shen stuffed her new clothes into the pots. She concealed her one silk slipper, too. She changed into her rags and waited for her stepmother to return.

Meanwhile, a traveler found the silk slipper on the road. He knew it was valuable, so he gave it to the king. The king was curious to find the owner of the slipper, so he had his men build a hut. Anyone could come to this hut to try on the silk slipper.

Yeh-Shen heard about the hut. She wanted her slipper back, so she sneaked out of the cave one night and ran quietly to the hut. As she crept toward the slipper, the king's men grabbed her.

The king took one look at Yeh-Shen's rags and thought she was a thief.

Yeh-Shen looked up at the king. Her eyes were filled with tears. The king saw how gentle and kind she was. He listened to her words.

"Please, I will show you the other slipper," Yeh-Shen whispered to the king.

Yeh-Shen led the king to her home. She put on the matching silk slipper and her fine clothes. The king knew then that he wanted to marry her. However, he was angry at how Jin and Jun-li had treated Yeh-Shen. He told them never to come to his castle, so they stayed in their cave for the rest of their lives.

**ANALYZE THE TEXT**

**Sequence of Events** What happened first, next, and last to Yeh-Shen? What lesson can you learn from these events?

# Dig Deeper

## Use Clues to Analyze the Text

Use these pages to learn about Sequence of Events and Comparing and Contrasting. Then read *Yeh-Shen* again. Use what you learn to understand it better.

## Sequence of Events

*Yeh-Shen* is about events that happen to a young girl. The events in the story happen in order. Thinking about the **sequence of events** can help you figure out the lesson in the story. Think about what happens and what the characters learn from the events. Then think about the lesson you can learn.

As you read, use a chart like the one below to help you retell the order of events.

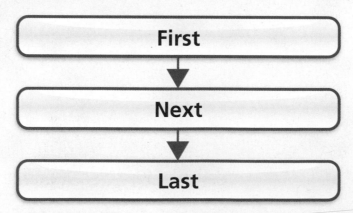

First

↓

Next

↓

Last

# Compare and Contrast

When you read a story, you can compare and contrast. When you **compare** and **contrast,** you tell how things are alike and different.

As you read *Yeh-Shen*, you can compare and contrast how the characters look, think, and act. You can also compare and contrast to see how the characters change in the story. This will help you see how the characters respond to story events and can help you understand more about them.

# Your Turn

 **What can you learn from reading a fairy tale?** Discuss the events in *Yeh-Shen* with a small group. Use text evidence to explain the story's lesson. Add your own ideas to what others say.

 **Classroom Conversation**

Now talk about these questions with the class.

1. In what ways does Yeh-Shen change in the story? In what ways does she stay the same?

2. Why does the king think Yeh-Shen is a thief?

3. Think about the end of the story. How might the king have treated Jin and Jun-li differently if they had been kind to Yeh-Shen?

### WRITE ABOUT READING

**Response** How do you think Yeh-Shen's stepmother and stepsister feel at the end of the story? Write a few sentences to explain your answer.

## Writing Tip

Use interesting and exact words to tell about the characters' feelings.

# Cinderella

by Sheila Sweeny Higginson

illustrated by Donald Wu

Once upon a time, there lived a girl named Cinderella. Cinderella was smart, kind, and beautiful. Her father loved her very much, and she loved him.

Cinderella had a stepmother and two stepsisters, too. They did not love Cinderella. They were jealous of her and were never kind.

Cinderella had to do all of the chores. She mopped
the floors and washed all of the dirty dishes. She dusted,
scrubbed, and polished every single thing in the house.
One day, Cinderella's family received an invitation to a ball.
The prince was having a dance and inviting all of the young
women in the kingdom.

Cinderella ironed her stepsisters' dresses. She brushed their
hair and fixed their bows. Then she waved good-bye as they
skipped off to the ball. Cinderella was not allowed to go.
After everyone left the house, Cinderella sat alone by the
fireplace and cried. Tears streamed down her beautiful face.
"Oh, how I wish that I could go to the ball," Cinderella
sobbed. "I wish that I had a beautiful dress to wear."

Just then, a tiny woman with wings flew through the window. She had a wand in her hand. It was Cinderella's fairy godmother! "Why are you crying, my dear?" the fairy godmother asked Cinderella.

"I want to go to the ball, too," cried Cinderella.

"Then you shall go!" said the fairy godmother.

Cinderella's fairy godmother waved her wand quickly in the air. Poof! A pumpkin transformed into a golden coach. Six mice turned into a team of horses to pull the coach. Whoosh! Cinderella's old, worn-out clothes were changed into a beautiful pink and silver gown and two glass slippers.

"What are you waiting for?" the fairy godmother asked Cinderella. "You need to get to the ball! Just make sure that you come home by midnight."

The prince saw Cinderella as soon as she entered the ballroom. He could not believe his eyes. She was the most beautiful girl he had ever seen.

The prince asked Cinderella to dance. The prince soon discovered that Cinderella was smart and kind, and he fell completely in love with her. Cinderella learned that the prince was good and noble. Cinderella fell in love with him, too.

Soon enough, the clock began to strike midnight in the
ballroom. Cinderella gasped and turned to race out of the
castle. As she ran out, one of her glass slippers fell off her
foot. Cinderella did not stop to get it.

The prince rushed after Cinderella, but he couldn't
catch her. He picked up the glass slipper and sighed. It
belonged on the foot of the girl he loved. He vowed to find
Cinderella and marry her.

The prince was true to his word. With the glass slipper in hand, he knocked on every door in the kingdom. He was looking for the girl whose foot would fit into the slipper.

Every girl wished the slipper would fit, especially Cinderella's stepsisters. The stepsisters tugged and pulled on the slipper. They pushed with all their might, but they could not fit their big feet into the slipper.

Cinderella watched her stepsisters as she stood next to the fireplace. At last, she stepped out so that the prince could see her.

"May I try?" she asked shyly.

The prince knelt down in front of Cinderella and held out the glass slipper. Cinderella placed her foot into the slipper, and it fit her perfectly. However, the prince did not need to see that. He looked into Cinderella's eyes. He knew that she was his true love.

The prince took Cinderella back to his castle, and they were married the next day. Then Cinderella, who was always kind, invited her father, her stepmother, and her stepsisters to live with the prince and her in the castle. They all lived happily ever after.

# Compare Texts

## TEXT TO TEXT

**Discuss Stories** Think about *Yeh-Shen* and *Cinderella*. How are the stories alike and different? Compare and contrast the characters, the settings, and the events. Discuss your ideas with a partner. Then tell which story you like better and why.

## TEXT TO SELF

**Make Decisions** Yeh-Shen sneaks out of the cave at night to get her lost slipper. Why is this not a safe thing to do? What would you do? Write to explain.

## TEXT TO WORLD

**Connect to Social Studies** *Yeh-Shen* is a fairy tale from China. Work with a partner to find three facts about China in a reference book. Write each fact on a sheet of paper. Draw a picture to go with each fact.

ELA RL.2.7, RL.2.9, W.2.7

# Grammar

**Possessive Nouns** A **possessive noun** shows that a person or animal owns or has something. Add an **apostrophe** (') and -*s* to a singular noun to make it a possessive noun. Add just an apostrophe to a plural noun that ends in -*s* to make it a possessive noun.

| Singular Possessive Nouns | Plural Possessive Nouns |
|---|---|
| one girl's shoe | many girls' shoes |
| a prince's festival | two princes' festivals |
| a king's horse | five kings' horses |

**Try This!** **Write each possessive noun correctly by adding an apostrophe (') or an apostrophe and -*s* to the name of the owner.**

❶ Yeh-Shen friend

❷ two sisters dresses

❸ a king castle

Use possessive nouns in your writing. They can help you avoid wordy sentences.

| Wordy Sentence | Sentence with Possessive Noun |
|---|---|
| The coach belonging to the girl was made from a pumpkin. | The girl's coach was made from a pumpkin. |

## Connect Grammar to Writing

**When you revise your response paragraph, look for places where you can use a possessive noun to fix a wordy sentence.**

# Opinion Writing

☑ **Evidence** When you write a **response paragraph,** use only details that support your opinions. Connect your opinions with reasons using linking words such as *and, because,* and *also.*

Arianna drafted a **response paragraph** about *Yeh-Shen.* Later, she revised her draft by taking out a detail that didn't belong and by adding linking words.

## Writing Checklist

☑ **Purpose**
Did I clearly state my opinion?

☑ **Organization**
Did I begin by stating my opinion?

☑ **Evidence**
Do all of my details link to my opinion?

☑ **Conventions**
Did I combine sentences that have the same subject?

## Revised Draft

I think the king was right to never allow Yeh-Shen's stepfamily into the castle again. Yeh-Shen's stepmother, Jin, was very mean
_because_
to her. Jin was angry. She made Yeh-Shen wear rags and work
_Also,_
all the time. Yeh-Shen was not allowed to have friends. ~~Her only friend had golden eyes.~~

# A Good Decision
## by Arianna Gerard

I think the king was right to never allow Yeh-Shen's stepfamily into the castle again. Yeh-Shen's stepmother, Jin, was very mean to her because Jin was angry. She made Yeh-Shen wear rags and work all the time. Also, Yeh-Shen was not allowed to have friends. Jun-li was not kind either. She was lazy and did not help Yeh-Shen. Jin and Jun-li needed to be punished because they treated Yeh-Shen so badly.

## Reading as a Writer

**Which detail did Arianna take out? Are there details you should take out of your paragraph?**

I took out a detail that didn't connect to my opinion.

## 🔍 LANGUAGE DETECTIVE

**Talk About Words**
Work with a partner. Choose one of the sentences. Take out the Vocabulary word. Put in a word that means the same or almost the same thing. Tell how the sentences are the same and how they are different.

# Vocabulary in Context

► **Study each Context Card.**

► **Place the Vocabulary words in alphabetical order.**

**1**    **search**

It is fun to search for buried treasure. You never know what you will find!

**2**    **contained**

This old box contained jewels, coins, and other treasures.

**3 startled**

The diver was startled to find treasure at the bottom of the ocean.

**4 odd**

Do you think it is odd, or strange, to look for buried treasure?

**5 leaned**

The woman leaned over to get a better view of the whale near the ship.

**6 tossed**

They tossed the supplies into the trunk to pack for their vacation.

**7 grateful**

The museum was very grateful, or thankful, to get the old statues.

**8 village**

This village is near the ocean. People find coins buried on the beach.

# Read and Comprehend

✓ **TARGET SKILL**

**Understanding Characters** Think about how characters act when something important happens to them. Think about what they say, do, and think. These details give text evidence to help you understand more about them. You can write text evidence about characters in a chart like this one.

| Character | What Happens | Words, Actions, Thoughts |
|-----------|--------------|--------------------------|
|           |              |                          |

✓ **TARGET STRATEGY**

**Summarize** As you read, stop to tell important ideas in your own words.

**ELA** RL.2.3, RL.2.7, SL.2.1a

## Traditional Stories

Traditional stories have been told for many years. Long ago, stories were told aloud and then retold. Now most stories are written down. People everywhere can read them. Traditional stories often are told to teach a lesson.

In *Two of Everything*, the characters learn an important lesson.

### Think | Pair | Share

Think about if it is better for stories to be written down or shared through speaking. Discuss your opinion with a partner. Then share your opinions with classmates.

*Two of Everything*

☑ **GENRE**

A **folktale** is a story that is often told by people of a country. As you read, look for:

▸ a simple plot that teaches a lesson
▸ events that could not happen in real life

**MEET THE AUTHOR AND ILLUSTRATOR**

# Lily Toy Hong

Lily Toy Hong enjoys camping, getting together with her large family, and eating Chinese food. She also loves learning about her parents' native country, China, and its many legends and folktales. "One day I would love to visit China and explore the land of my forefathers," she says, "and maybe discover more folktales."

# Two of Everything

## by Lily Toy Hong

**ESSENTIAL QUESTION**

What good things happen when people work together?

Once long ago, in a humble little hut, lived Mr. Haktak and his wife, Mrs. Haktak. They were old and very poor. What little they ate came from their tiny garden.

In a lucky year when the harvest was plentiful,
Mr. Haktak had a little extra to take to the village.
There he traded turnips, potatoes, and other
vegetables for clothing, lamp oil, and fresh seeds.

One spring morning when Mr. Haktak was digging in his garden, his shovel struck something hard. Puzzled, he dug deeper into the dark ground until he came upon an ancient pot made of brass.

"How odd," said Mr. Haktak to himself. "To think that I have been digging here all these years and never came upon this pot before! I will take it home. Maybe Mrs. Haktak can find some use for it."

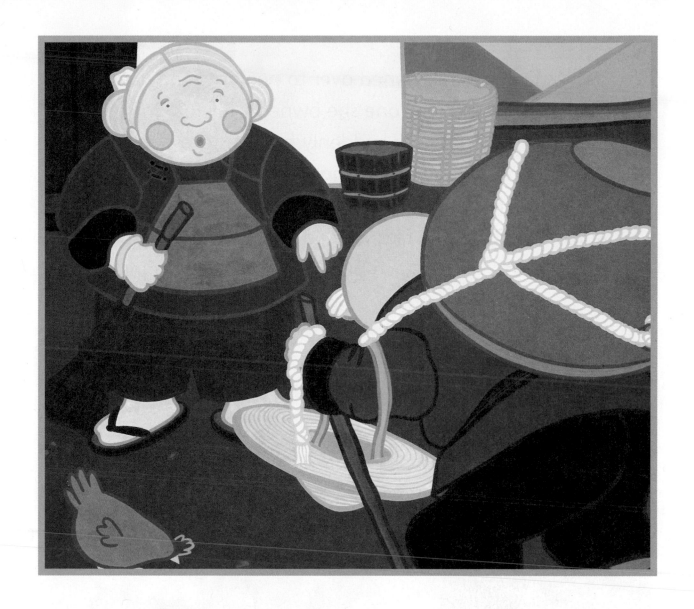

The pot was big and heavy for old Mr. Haktak.
As he stumbled along, his purse, which contained his
last five gold coins, fell to the ground. He tossed it
into the pot for safekeeping and staggered home.

His wife greeted him at the door. "Dear husband,
what a strange pot!" Mr. Haktak explained how he
found the pot. "I wonder what we can do with it,"
said Mrs. Haktak. "It looks too large to cook in and
too small to bathe in."

As Mrs. Haktak leaned over to peer into the pot, her hairpin—the only one she owned—fell in. She felt around in the pot, and suddenly her eyes grew round with surprise. "Look!" she shouted. "I've pulled out TWO hairpins, exactly alike, and TWO purses, too!" Sure enough, the purses were identical, and so were the hairpins. Inside each purse were five gold coins!

Mr. Haktak was so excited he jumped up and down. "Let's put my winter coat inside the pot. If we are lucky again the pot will make two coats, and then we will both stay warm." So into the pot went one coat—and out came TWO coats.

They began to search the house and quickly put more things into the magical pot. "If only we had some meat," wished Mr. Haktak, "or fresh fruit, or one delicious sweet cake."

Mrs. Haktak smiled. "I know how we can get anything we want," she said. She put their ten coins into one purse, then threw it into the pot. She pulled out two purses with ten coins in each.

"What a clever wife I have!" cried Mr. Haktak. "Each time we do this we will have twice as much money as before!"

The Haktaks worked late into the night, filling and emptying the pot until the floor was covered with coins.

---

**ANALYZE THE TEXT**

**Understanding Characters** Do you agree with Mr. Haktak that his wife is clever? Explain.

Morning came, and off went Mr. Haktak with a long list of things to buy in the village. Instead of vegetables, his basket was full of gold coins.

Mrs. Haktak finished all of her chores and sat down to enjoy a cup of tea. She sipped her tea and admired the brass pot. Then with a grateful heart, she knelt and embraced it. "Dear pot, I do not know where you came from, but you are my best friend." She stooped over the pot to look inside.

At that very moment, Mr. Haktak returned. His arms were so full of packages that he had to kick the door open. Bang! Mrs. Haktak was so startled that she lost her balance and fell headfirst into the pot!

Mr. Haktak ran over and grabbed his wife's legs. He pulled and tugged until she slid out onto the floor. But when he looked at the pot again, he gasped. Two more legs were sticking straight out of it! Naturally, he took hold of the ankles and pulled.

Out came a second person! She looked exactly like his wife.

The new Mrs. Haktak sat silently on the floor looking lost. But the first Mrs. Haktak cried, "I am your one and only wife! Put that woman back into the pot right now!"

Mr. Haktak yelled, "No! If I put her back we will not have two women but THREE. One wife is enough for me!"

He backed away from his angry wife, and tripped and fell headfirst into the pot himself!

**ANALYZE THE TEXT**

**Point of View** What story details do you learn from the person telling the story? Which details do you learn from what Mr. Haktak says?

497

Both Mrs. Haktaks rushed to rescue him. Each grasped an ankle, and together they pulled him out. There were two more legs in the pot. So they pulled out the other Mr. Haktak, too.

"Just what use does one Mr. Haktak have for another!" Mr. Haktak cried angrily. "This pot is not as wonderful as we thought it to be. Now even our troubles are beginning to double."

But his wife had been thinking while he was yelling.

"Calm down," she said. "It is good that the other Mrs. Haktak has her own Mr. Haktak. Perhaps we will become best of friends. After all, we are so alike he will be a brother to you and she a sister to me. With our pot we can make two of everything, so there will be plenty to go around."

And that is what they did.  The Haktaks built two fine new homes.  Each house had identical teapots, rice bowls, silk embroideries, and bamboo furniture.

From the outside, the houses looked exactly alike, but there was one difference.  Hidden in one house was a big brass pot.  Of course, the Haktaks were always very careful not to fall into it again!

The new Haktaks and the old Haktaks did become good friends. The neighbors thought that the Haktaks had grown so rich that they decided to have two of everything—even themselves!

# Dig Deeper

## Use Clues to Analyze the Text

Use these pages to learn about Understanding Characters and Point of View. Then read *Two of Everything* again. Use what you learn to understand it better.

## Understanding Characters

*Two of Everything* tells how the Haktaks' pot creates a problem. Think about what the characters do and say and how they respond to events in the story. This can help you understand what they are like. For example, on page 490, Mr. Haktak finds the pot and takes it home. This shows that he wants it to be used for something.

Use the chart below to list text evidence about what happens and how the characters react.

| Character | What Happens | Words, Actions, Thoughts |
|-----------|--------------|--------------------------|
|           |              |                          |

# Point of View

Characters may not think about the same event in the same way. One character may be upset about an event. Another character might be happy about the same event. The way that a character thinks about something is called his or her **point of view.**

When you read a story aloud, think about each character's point of view. This will help you know what kind of voice to use when you read each character's words. Use a different voice as you read to show each character's point of view.

# Your Turn

**What good things happen when people work together?** Think about what the characters in the story do when they have a problem. What happens when they work together to solve the problem? Share your ideas with a partner using text evidence from *Two of Everything.* Take turns talking.

## Classroom Conversation

Now talk about these questions with the class.

1. How do the characters' feelings change throughout the story?

2. What lessons did Mr. and Mrs. Haktak learn? Use text evidence to support your answer.

3. How could the Haktaks use their pot to help others?

ELA RL.2.1, RL.2.2, RL.2.3, W.2.1, SL.2.1a

### WRITE ABOUT READING

**Response** Think about the story. Do you think that Mrs. Haktak's idea to make two of everything was a good one? Write an opinion paragraph. Use text evidence to support your opinion. Use linking words such as *because* to connect your opinion to your reasons.

## Writing Tip

Remember that pronouns can take the place of nouns. Use a pronoun instead of using the same noun over and over.

# TRADITIONAL TALE

## ✅ GENRE

**Traditional tales** are stories that have been told for many years.

## ✅ TEXT FOCUS

A **folktale** is a story passed down to explain or entertain.

## Readers' Theater

# Stone Soup

adapted by
Greta McLaughlin

| Cast of Characters | | |
| --- | --- | --- |
| Narrator | Traveler | Boy |

**Narrator:** A hungry man set out to search for food. He stopped in a village and knocked on the door of every home.

**Traveler:** Please, could you share some food with me?

**Narrator:** It startled the villagers to see a stranger. They would not share with him.

**Narrator:** The man leaned against a well. He took a pot out of his sack and filled it with water.

**Boy:** What are you doing?

**Traveler:** I've tossed a stone into my pot so I can make stone soup.

**Boy:** That's odd. Is stone soup good?

**Traveler:** It is. But the soup would be better if I had a carrot.

**Boy:** Grandma grows carrots. I'll ask her for one.

**Traveler:** Thank you. Please, ask her to join us for soup.

**Narrator:** The boy stopped at all the villagers' homes. He gathered food to put into the pot. Soon the soup contained carrots, green beans, potatoes, and more.

**Boy:** Is the soup ready?

**Traveler:** Yes, it is just right.

**Narrator:** The man shared his soup with the grateful villagers. In turn, they made sure that he never went hungry again.

  # Compare Texts

## TEXT TO TEXT

**Have a Discussion** Imagine that the traveler in *Stone Soup* came to the Haktaks' village. What do you think the Haktaks would do if the traveler asked them to help him make soup? Talk about your ideas with a small group. Use text evidence from both stories to help you.

## TEXT TO SELF

**Write a Paragraph** What do the Haktaks do when they find the magical pot? Would you do the same thing? Write to explain.

## TEXT TO WORLD

**Connect to Traditional Tales** Read another version of *Stone Soup*. Compare and contrast the two stories. How are the settings, characters, and events the same? How are they different?

ELA RL.2.1, RL.2.7, RL.2.9

# Grammar

**Possessive Pronouns**  A **possessive pronoun** is a **pronoun** that shows ownership.  The possessive pronouns *my* and *your* are used before nouns.  The possessive pronouns *mine* and *yours* are used after nouns.  *His* can be used before or after nouns.

| Pronouns Used Before Nouns | Pronouns Used After Nouns |
| --- | --- |
| My purse is new. | The new purse is mine. |
| Jess has your small pot. | The small pot is yours. |
| His house is the biggest. | The biggest house is his. |

 **Work with a partner.  Read each sentence aloud.  Name the possessive pronouns.**

❶ Carmen showed the big pot to her class.

❷ I couldn't believe my eyes.

❸ Mark said the big pot was his.

❹ I wanted the big pot to be mine!

You can use possessive pronouns in place of repeated possessive nouns. This can make your writing clearer.

| Repeated Possessive Noun | Possessive Pronoun |
| --- | --- |
| Sal said that the twins were brothers of Sal's. | Sal said that the twins were brothers of hers. |

## Connect Grammar to Writing

As you revise your response essay next week, look for possessive nouns that you can change to possessive pronouns. This will make your writing smoother.

# Opinion Writing

✅ **Evidence** When you write a **response to literature,** include reasons for your opinion. Give examples to support each of your reasons.

Cooper planned his essay in response to *Two of Everything.* He thought of reasons for his opinion. Then he used an opinion chart to add examples.

## Writing Process Checklist

▶ **Prewrite**

✓ **Did I identify my opinion about this story?**

✓ **Did I give reasons for my opinion?**

✓ **Did I come up with good examples for each of my reasons?**

**Draft**

**Revise**

**Edit**

**Publish and Share**

### Exploring a Topic

The pot was good for the Haktaks. Why?

| Reason 1: | Reason 2: |
|---|---|
| The pot doubled everything for them. | They ended up happy after all. |

## Opinion Chart

My Opinion: The pot was good for the Haktaks.

| | |
|---|---|
| **Reason 1:** The pot doubled everything for them. | **Reason 2:** They ended up happy after all. |
| **Example 1:** Mr. Haktak put his coins in the pot, and it doubled his money. | **Example 1:** The pot gave them a second home and everything to put in it. |
| **Example 2:** The pot gave them a second Mr. and Mrs. Haktak. | **Example 2:** They made friends with the new Mr. and Mrs. Haktak. |

## Reading as a Writer

What examples did Cooper add to support his reasons? Which examples can you give to support your opinion?

I gave reasons and examples to support my opinion.

## 🔍 LANGUAGE DETECTIVE

**Talk About Words**
Work with a partner.
Take turns asking and
answering questions
about the photos. Use
the Vocabulary words
in your questions and
answers.

# Vocabulary in Context

▶ Study each **Context Card**.

▶ Use the Vocabulary words to tell a story about two of the pictures.

**1** **inventions**
Wheels are one of the
inventions that we use in
many different ways.

**2** **remarkable**
The telephone is a
remarkable invention that
lets you talk to people.

### 3 designed

These boys designed and built a truck from blocks that snap together.

### 4 amounts

These light bulbs give off different amounts of light.

### 5 accomplishments

One of Ben Franklin's many accomplishments was bifocal glasses to see near and far.

### 6 achieve

Wanting to succeed helped Ben achieve, or reach, his goals. This is a statue of Ben.

### 7 composed

Beethoven is famous for the beautiful music he composed, or wrote.

### 8 result

When a musician plays the armonica, beautiful music is the result!

# Read and Comprehend

**Compare and Contrast** Authors sometimes **compare** two things, or tell how they are the same. They also sometimes **contrast** two things, or tell how they are different.

Authors may give details to compare and contrast places, things, events, or ideas. You can use text evidence and a diagram like the one below to compare and contrast.

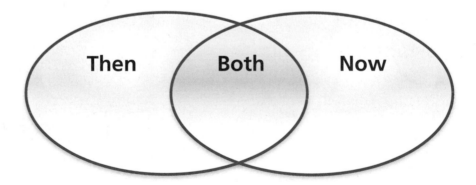

Then | Both | Now

✓ **TARGET STRATEGY**

**Visualize** As you read, picture in your mind what is happening to help you understand and remember important ideas and details.

## Historical Figures and Documents

There are many people who lived in the past that are still important today. Some people from long ago are important because they helped the United States become a country. Some wrote documents that are still used today. A **document** is a piece of paper that has something important written on it. The Constitution is an example of a document from long ago. It is a set of rules for our country that helps people make laws today.

In *Now & Ben*, you will learn more about Benjamin Franklin. He lived long ago and was a great inventor. He also helped write important documents.

**Think | Write | Pair | Share**

Write two rules you would make if you were in charge of the country. Share them with a partner. Choose two rules you both feel are the most important and share with the class.

*Now & Ben*
*The Modern Inventions of Benjamin Franklin*

GENE BARRETTA

☑ **GENRE**

**Informational text**
gives facts about a topic.
As you read, look for:

▶ pictures that help
  explain the topic
▶ information about real
  events and people

**MEET THE AUTHOR
AND ILLUSTRATOR**

# Gene Barretta

Benjamin Franklin is one
of Gene Barretta's heroes.
Like his hero, Mr. Barretta
is a writer and makes his
home in Philadelphia,
Pennsylvania. He even
named his son Benjamin.

Sometimes when Mr.
Barretta visits schools to
talk about his book *Now
& Ben*, an actor dressed as
Benjamin Franklin goes
with him.

# Now & Ben
## The Modern Inventions of Ben Franklin

FRANKLIN

DIPLOMAT

TRAVELER

HUMOR

NTER

written and illustrated by
Gene Barretta

## ESSENTIAL QUESTION

Why might a person
from long ago still be
important today?

**Now and then,** we think about Ben.
Dr. Benjamin Franklin, to be precise. And we
think about his many inventions—inventions he
originated more than two hundred years ago.

It was as if Ben could see into the future. Almost
everything he created is still around today. For
instance . . .

# Now...

our newspapers are filled with illustrations.

# Ben...

was the first to print a political cartoon in America.
The cartoon encouraged the American colonies to join
together or die like the disconnected snake.

# Now...

our world relies on electricity. In the eighteenth century, many people believed that lightning was an act of anger and punishment from God.

# Ben...

was one of the scientists who discovered the true nature of electricity and how to use it. He learned that lightning is electricity when he attached a small metal wire to the top of a kite and gathered electricity from a storm cloud.

# Now...

many buildings and homes use lightning rods to protect against lightning strikes.

# Ben...

invented the lightning rod and was the first to use it. The pointed iron rod acts like a magnet and grabs an approaching lightning bolt from the sky before it can strike the rooftop. The electricity then travels safely down a long wire into the ground. It prevents fires and keeps dangerous amounts of electricity away from the house.

## ANALYZE THE TEXT

**Using Context** What is a lightning rod? How do the words and illustrations help you understand its purpose?

525

# NOW...

this gadget goes by many names, such as the Grabber. Everyone has seen one—it's the long stick that helps grab items from out-of-reach places.

526

# Ben...

invented the original device and called it the Long Arm because it worked like a very long arm.

**ANALYZE THE TEXT**

**Compare and Contrast** What about this invention is the same today as it was when Ben invented it? What is different about it?

# Now...

swimmers and divers use flippers to move faster through the water.

# Now...

ships travel across the Gulf Stream to take advantage of the faster current.

# Now...

we understand and accept the benefits of vitamin C.

# Ben...

invented things even when he was a boy. He was an avid swimmer and built wooden flippers for both his hands and feet.

# Ben...

measured, charted, and publicized the Gulf Stream during his eight voyages across the Atlantic Ocean.

# Ben...

was an early promoter of eating citrus fruits to help prevent a disease called scurvy.

Now...

for a musical interlude.

# Ben...

invented the glass armonica. He was able to create music by simply touching his wet fingers to a row of spinning glass bowls. Mozart and Beethoven were so moved by the sounds that they composed for the instrument.

Today, glass armonicas are very rare. You are more likely to find one in a museum than in a music store.

TUNED GLASS BOWLS TURN ON A ROD

WHEEL TURNS THE GLASS BOWLS →

TUNED GLASS BOWLS

FOOT PEDAL MAKES THE WHEEL TURN

ARMONICA

# Now...

chairs come in all shapes and sizes.

# Ben...

designed two chairs that are still very useful. The writing chair combined a desk and chair into one. The library chair was a combination chair and stepladder.

# Now...

everyone has seen a rocking chair, but not many have seen Dr. Franklin's rocking chairs.

# Ben...

invented one rocking chair with a fan on top and one that churned butter.

# NOW...

every year, we observe daylight saving time, which means we set our clocks ahead one hour in the springtime. As a result, it stays darker longer in the morning when most people are sleeping and stays light longer at the end of the day so we can save more energy. In the fall, we return the clocks to standard time.

# Ben...

suggested this idea in one of his essays as a way to save money by burning fewer candles. Farmers could also gain more work time in the evening. Daylight saving time was not officially practiced until World War I, more than a hundred years later.

As for clocks . . .
Ben designed the first clock with a second hand.

# Now...

every automobile has an odometer to measure the distance it travels.

# Ben...

invented the odometer when he was postmaster general so he could measure his postal routes.

# Now...

almost every large community includes a library, a hospital, a post office, a fire department, and a sanitation department.

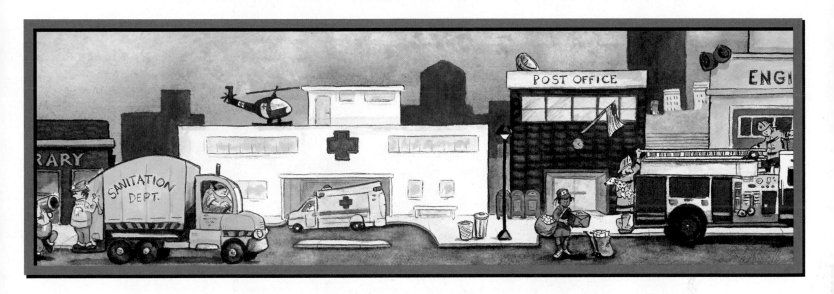

# Ben...

lived in a city that had none of these establishments, so he helped organize the first of each.

**Now...** and then, we owe thanks to Ben for his important inventions. But many would agree that his greatest accomplishments came in the form of documents—documents that helped shape the world.

536

**Ben...** had a pivotal role in developing America's Constitution, the Treaty of Alliance with France, the Treaty of Peace with England, and the Declaration of Independence. It's remarkable that one man could achieve so much in a lifetime. He has certainly helped to form the modern world. . . .

Will his contributions help to form the future?

538

# Dig Deeper

## Use Clues to Analyze the Text

Use these pages to learn about Comparing and Contrasting and Using Context. Then read *Now & Ben* again. Use what you learn to understand it better.

## Compare and Contrast

In *Now & Ben*, the author compares and contrasts things from the past and things from today. To **compare** and **contrast** means to tell how things are the same and different.

As you reread, use text evidence to compare and contrast how things were in the past to how they are today. This can help you connect events from the past to your life today. Use a diagram like the one below to help you compare and contrast.

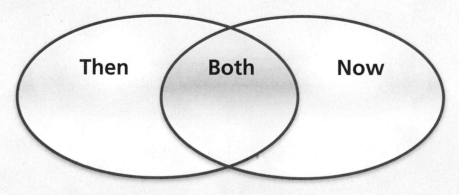

Then        Both        Now

# Using Context

Authors sometimes use words and phrases that you might not know. You can use the other words in the sentence to help you figure out the meaning. You can also look at the pictures. The pictures are text evidence that give clues about what a word or phrase means. When you use words and pictures to figure out the meaning, it is called **using context.**

# Your Turn

**Turn and Talk**

**Why might a person from long ago still be important today?** Share your ideas with a partner. Include text evidence from *Now & Ben.* Then listen carefully to your partner's ideas.

**Classroom Conversation**

Now talk about these questions with the class.

1. How does learning about history help people understand life today?

2. How is life today different from when Ben Franklin was alive? Explain using text evidence.

3. What might Ben Franklin say if he could see how his ideas are being used today?

**WRITE ABOUT READING** ··································

**Response** Ben Franklin had many inventions and did many important things. What do you think is the most important thing that he did in his life? Why? Write a short paragraph to explain your answer.

### Writing Tip

A possessive noun shows a person owns something. Remember to use an apostrophe to form a possessive noun.

# INFORMATIONAL TEXT

A Model
Citizen

☑ **GENRE**

**Informational text** gives facts about a topic. This is a social studies text.

☑ **TEXT FOCUS**

**Formal language** is used when writing or speaking in school or with someone you don't know well.
**Informal language** is used when writing or speaking to friends or family members.

# A Model Citizen

Ben Franklin became famous for many reasons. He spent large amounts of his time doing scientific experiments. He designed new inventions. He owned a newspaper and composed many stories for it.

Franklin was a good citizen. He began the first fire company in America. He also started the first public library. As a result, life was better for people.

In 1776, Great Britain had colonies in America. People in the colonies wanted to be free. They fought the Revolutionary War against Britain to become free.

The colonists asked Franklin to help them achieve freedom. He helped Thomas Jefferson write the Declaration of Independence. The thirteen colonies won the war in 1783 and became the United States of America.

## The Thirteen Original American Colonies

NEW HAMPSHIRE

MASSACHUSETTS

NEW YORK

RHODE ISLAND
CONNECTICUT

PENNSYLVANIA

NEW JERSEY

DELAWARE

MARYLAND

VIRGINIA

ATLANTIC OCEAN

NORTH CAROLINA

SOUTH CAROLINA

GEORGIA

After the war, Franklin helped to write a plan for the government of the United States. This plan was called the Constitution of the United States.

Ben Franklin had a life full of remarkable accomplishments. He is a model for us all.

This painting shows the signing of the Declaration of Independence. Franklin is standing beside Thomas Jefferson.

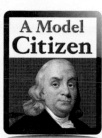

# Compare Texts

**Compare and Contrast** *Now & Ben* and *A Model Citizen* are both about Benjamin Franklin. With a partner, make a list of the most important ideas about him from each selection. Then talk about how the information in each selection is the same and different.

**Write a Poem** Think about Ben Franklin's inventions and what he did for our country when it was new. Write a poem to tell how you feel about what he did.

With Ben's fins,
you will swim fast.
In a race,
you will never be last.

**Connect to Social Studies** Tell how Ben Franklin helped his community. How do the things Ben did for his community make our lives better today? Share your ideas with the class.

ELA RI.2.3, RI.2.9

# Grammar

**Choosing Between Adjectives and Adverbs** An **adjective** is a word that describes a noun. An **adverb** is a word that describes a verb. Choose to use an adjective or an adverb depending on the word being described.

| Sentence | Part of Speech | Describing Word |
|---|---|---|
| Ben Franklin was a ____ man. | noun | smart |
| He ____ worked for the people. | verb | bravely |
| Ben Franklin invented ____ things. | noun | many |
| He ____ flew a kite in a storm. | verb | carefully |

**Try This!** **Work with a partner to choose a word from the box to complete each sentence.**

| often | useful | brave | proudly |
|---|---|---|---|

❶ Many _____ inventions were made by Ben.

❷ Ben _____ signed the Declaration of Independence.

❸ He _____ worked to invent new things.

❹ He was a _____ role model.

Use adjectives and adverbs correctly in your writing. This will make your writing more exact, and it will sound better to the reader.

| Incorrect | Correct |
| --- | --- |
| Tim thought **good** of Ben Franklin. | Tim thought **well** of Ben Franklin. |

## Connect Grammar to Writing

**When you revise your response essay, check that adjectives describe nouns and that adverbs describe verbs.**

# Opinion Writing

✓ **Elaboration** When you write a **response to literature,** use words that show your opinion.

Cooper wrote a draft of his essay in response to *Two of Everything*. Later, he revised his draft by adding some opinion words and phrases.

## Writing Process Checklist

**Prewrite**

**Draft**

▶ **Revise**

✓ **Did I tell things in the order they happen in the story?**

✓ **Did I use opinion words and phrases?**

✓ **Did I sum up my reasons at the end?**

**Edit**

**Publish and Share**

### Revised Draft

The Haktaks were better off

with their special pot. At first

                    terrible
it seemed like a ∧ problem. Then
the problems turned into good
~~things changed.~~
∧                                      fortune.

The pot doubled everything for

the Haktaks. It doubled their

money. When Mr. Haktak put coins

in the pot, he got twice the money. ∧

That was wonderful!

# The Special Pot Was a Good Thing
## by Cooper Jackson

The Haktaks were better off with their special pot. At first it seemed like a terrible problem. Then the problems turned into good fortune.

The pot doubled everything for the Haktaks. It doubled their money. When Mr. Haktak put coins in the pot, he got twice the money. That was wonderful!

The pot gave a second Mr. and Mrs. Haktak. The pot also gave a second home.

## Reading as a Writer

How did the words Cooper added show his opinion? Which opinion words and phrases can you add to your essay?

I added opinion words and phrases to my essay.

# Write an Opinion Essay

**TASK** Look back at *The Mysterious Tadpole*.
What do you like about the story? What do you
dislike? Write an essay explaining your opinion
of the story for other children to read.

**PLAN** · · · · · · · · · · · · · · · · · · · · · · · · · · · · · · · · · · · · · · ▤ myNotebook

Use the tools in
your eBook to
remember
details from
*The Mysterious
Tadpole.*

**Gather Information** Talk with a partner about
*The Mysterious Tadpole*. Answer questions like
these:

- What happens in the story that you like?

- What happens in the story that you do not
  like?

- Who is your favorite or least favorite
  character? Why?

- Do you like the ending?

In a web, write story details that support your
opinion of the story.

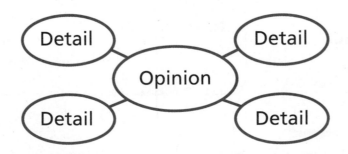

**DRAFT** ............................................................

Write your draft in *my*WriteSmart.

**Write Your Essay**  Use the information below to help you organize your essay.

## Opinion

Start with an opening sentence that tells your opinion about the story.  This is what you will explain to readers.

## Reasons

Write reasons that support your opinion. Use the chart you made and details from the story to help you.  Words such as *because*, *and*, or *also* can help you link your reasons to your opinion.  Use apostrophes correctly when you write possessive nouns.  Make sure you don't give away the ending of the story!

## Conclusion

Write a conclusion that repeats your opinion of the book in a different way.

553

**Review Your Draft**  Read your writing and make it better. Use the Checklist.

Have a partner read your draft. Talk about how you can make it better.

 Does my essay state my opinion of *The Mysterious Tadpole*?

 Did I connect my reasons to my opinion using words such as *because*, *and*, or *also*?

 Did I use details from the story to support my opinion?

 Did I use apostrophes correctly?

**PRESENT**

**Share**  Write or type a copy of your essay. Pick a way to share.

- Read your essay to your classmates.

- Make a class book of the essays to display or share with other classes.

Our Opinions of The Mysterious Tadpole

554

# Glossary

This glossary can help you find the meanings of some of the words in this book. The meanings given are the meanings of the words as they are used in the book. Sometimes a second meaning is also given.

# A

**accept**

To take what is given: *I accept your gift and would like to give you something too.*

**accepted**

A form of **accept:** *He accepted the package and waited until he was alone to open it.*

**accomplish**

To do completely, or carry out: *They accomplish the job by working together.*

**accomplishments**

A form of **accomplish:** *The concert showed the accomplishments of each musician.*

**account**

A record of money received or spent: *A savings account helps you keep track of money you put in the bank.*

**achieve**

To succeed in doing: *Some people achieve a lot by studying on the Internet.*

**agree**

To have the same idea or opinion: *I agree with you that it is a good day to go swimming.*

**agreed**

A form of **agree:** *The two friends agreed to meet at the bridge after school.*

### amaze

To surprise or to fill with wonder: *The huge redwood trees **amaze** many visitors.*

### amazed

A form of **amaze:** *We were **amazed** when we saw the first whale.*

### amounts

Quantity or sum of quantities: *Always measure the **amounts** of juice before you add them to the batter.*

**amount**

### answer

To say, write, or do something in reply: *When you **answer** the questions, write the numbers to go with them.*

### answered

A form of **answer:** *Nobody **answered** my call at first, but then I heard a tiny voice.*

### assistant

A helper, or one who assists: *He needed an **assistant** to work with the animals.*

# B

### blaze

To burn: *The sun may **blaze** too strongly for us to stay at the beach.*

### blazed

A form of **blaze:** *Our campfire **blazed** in the darkness and kept us warm all evening.*

### budget

A plan for how money will be spent: *Our family **budget** includes amounts for food, clothing, and heat.*

# C

**cage**

A space closed around with wire or bars: *Sometimes they shut all their windows and let the bird out of her* **cage**.

**cheer**

To shout in happiness or in praise: *Everybody will* **cheer** *and clap when the musicians take their bows.*

**cheered**

A form of **cheer:** *The crowd* **cheered** *when the mayor gave her the award.*

**chuckle**

To laugh quietly: *I sometimes* **chuckle** *when I think about the silly things we did.*

**chuckled**

A form of **chuckle:** *They* **chuckled** *at the comic strip in the newspaper.*

**clear**

To get rid of or remove: *After the storm, we will* **clear** *away the branches from the path.*

**cleared**

A form of **clear:** *When they* **cleared** *the table after the meal, they planned what to do next.*

**compose**

To create or make up: *He likes to* **compose** *songs for the musical each year.*

**composed**

A form of **compose:** *She* **composed** *a duet for flute and piano.*

**conceal**

To hide something so that it cannot be seen: *I tried to* **conceal** *the gift I bought for my aunt because I wanted to surprise her.*

### concealed

A form of **conceal:** *I concealed my diary in my closet so that my sister couldn't find it.*

### confuse

To mix up: *Sometimes people **confuse** twins who look very much alike.*

### confused

A form of **confuse:** *The cookies taste salty because he **confused** the sugar with the salt.*

### contain

To keep inside or hold: *Oranges **contain** vitamins and other things that are good for your health.*

### contained

A form of **contain:** *The box **contained** a new set of pencils.*

contained

### content

To be happy or satisfied: *The lazy cat is **content** to lie in the sun all morning.*

### control

To direct or be in charge of: *The children learned to **control** the hand puppets.*

### copy

To make something exactly like an original: *I will **copy** this picture in color so you can see the details.*

### curb

A stone rim along the edge of a sidewalk or road: *Workers are fixing the **curb** along this street.*

# D

### delicious

Tasting or smelling very good: *He made some vegetable soup that was **delicious**.*

## depend

To rely on or need for support:
*Dogs **depend** on their owners
to feed them.*

## depended

A form of **depend:** *The group
**depended** on her to lead the
way out of the forest.*

## design

To make a plan for: *We always
**design** furniture before we
build it.*

## designed

A form of **design:** *She
**designed** this desk to hold a
computer and a printer.*

## disappoint

To let down hopes or wishes:
*I don't want to **disappoint** my
parents, so I try to do my best
in school.*

## disappointed

A form of **disappoint:** *They
were **disappointed** that their
team did not make the
final round.*

## discover

To find out, or to find: *It is
exciting to **discover** a hidden
treasure.*

## discovered

A form of **discover:** *When she
**discovered** the shiny stones,
she showed them to her
teacher.*

## duplicate

To make an exact copy of: *It is
hard to **duplicate** a painting
with many details.*

## duplicated

A form of **duplicate:** *We
**duplicated** these pictures on
a copier.*

## dye

Something that gives or adds
color to cloth, paper, or other
material: *We colored shirts by
dipping them in **dye**.*

# E

## empty

Containing nothing: *The bottle is almost **empty**, but you can have the last few sips of water.*

## exact

Accurate in every detail: *He hoped to make an **exact** copy of the statue.*

## exercise

Activity that helps the body: *People and animals need **exercise** every day.*

## explain

To make clear or give reasons for: *If you **explain** what to do, I will try to do it.*

## explained

A form of **explain:** *After my father **explained** how the camera worked, I began to use it.*

## express

To make known: *Her stories **express** the feelings of the characters very well.*

## extra

More than what is usual or needed: *She made an **extra** loaf of bread to give to me.*

# F

## fail

To be unsuccessful: *We don't want to **fail** to reach the top of the mountain.*

## failed

A form of **fail:** *They **failed** to find the missing gloves, but at least they found the scarf.*

## final

Coming at the end: *We took a **final** spelling test at the end of the school year.*

## finally

At last, after a long while: ***Finally** the long car ride was over.*

### fling

Throw hard: *If I **fling** this rock into the water, it might skip over the waves.*

### flung

A form of **fling:** *She **flung** the ball so hard it went way past home plate and into the bleachers.*

### flutter

To flap, beat, or wave rapidly: *Moths **flutter** around the porch light in the evening.*

### fluttering

A form of **flutter:** *A hummingbird was **fluttering** around the bright garden flowers.*

**fluttering**

### fortune

The luck that comes to a person: *I had the good **fortune** to win a ticket to the big game.*

### fund

A sum of money raised or kept for a certain purpose: *The family has a vacation **fund** that helps them save for summer travel.*

# G

### gaze

To look for a long time: *We **gaze** in wonder at the snowy mountains.*

### gazing

A form of **gaze:** *They were **gazing** at the pink and purple clouds in the sunset sky.*

### glimmering

Shiny or sparkling: *The **glimmering** jewels are very beautiful.*

### grain

A very small part of something: *A **grain** of sand is so small that you can barely see it.*

### grand

Wonderful or important: *He felt **grand** when he marched in the parade.*

### grateful

Feeling thankful or showing thanks: *They were so **grateful** for her help that they gave her a gift.*

### growl

To make a low, deep, angry sound: *We don't want the bear to **growl** at us.*

### growled

A form of **growl**: *When the wolf **growled**, she jumped back.*

### guard

Someone who protects or watches over: *The **guard** kept watch all night long.*

### guess

To have or offer an idea without all the needed information: *I'll **guess** that there are about three hundred pennies in the jar.*

### guessed

A form of **guess**: *She **guessed** that the skates would still fit, but she would soon find out.*

# H

### heavily

A form of **heavy**: *The snow was falling so **heavily** that we had to shovel the path again.*

### heavy

Weighing a lot, thick, or hard to bear: *This is a **heavy** box for one person to carry.*

### hero

A person who is admired for brave, kind, or important actions: *She is a **hero** because she helped so many people find safety.*

## hurried

A form of **hurry:** *We all **hurried** inside because the rain got very heavy.*

## hurry

To act or move quickly: *Sometimes I **hurry** to get to the bus on time.*

# I

## inventions

Original machines, systems, or processes: *Radios, telephones, and cameras were important **inventions** in the past.*

**invention**

# J

## junior

Younger in a family or group: *The **junior** players learned from the senior players.*

# K

## knot

Tied-together piece of rope or string: *The **knot** was so tight that I had to cut the string.*

# L

## lean

To slant to one side or to rest on: *You can **lean** your head on my shoulder if you are sleepy.*

## leaned

A form of **lean:** *Some people **leaned** against the wall because there were no chairs left.*

## lonely

Sad about being alone or far from friends: *He felt **lonely** after his brother left for summer camp.*

# N

## nutrition

What our body gets from food in order to grow and stay healthy: *An orange is a food that has a lot of **nutrition**.*

# O

## odd

Unusual or strange: *The car was making an **odd** noise, so we stopped to check.*

## ordinary

Common, usual: *This bread you baked tastes better than **ordinary** bread.*

## otherwise

If not or if things were different: *I ran fast, because **otherwise** I would have missed the train.*

## overjoyed

A feeling of being very happy: *I was **overjoyed** to find out that my poem won first place.*

## overlook

To miss seeing, or not notice: *Please don't **overlook** the people who helped make costumes for the play.*

## overlooked

A form of **overlook:** *The smallest kitten was **overlooked** at first, but then we found him.*

# P

## peace

Calm: *If you want **peace** and quiet, try camping in the wilderness.*

## peacefully

A form of **peace:** *The cat dozed **peacefully** on the sofa.*

## plan

To decide on what to do: *We **plan** to travel all day.*

## planning

A form of **plan:** *If you are planning for the party, be sure to get balloons.*

## pod

A shell that covers some seeds: *You can eat some peas while they are still in their pod.*

## polite

Having or showing good manners: *Their parents showed them how to be polite.*

## position

Location, or area that a team player is assigned: *Some players wanted to change their position on the soccer team.*

## practice

To do over and over to gain skill: *I practice playing the drums twice a week.*

## pretend

To make believe or act as though something is true: *We are riding pretend horses when we ride our bikes.*

## prize

Something won in a contest: *The prize for the best dancers was a blue ribbon.*

prize

# R

## receive

To take or get something that is sent or given: *We receive many cards for the holiday every year.*

### received

A form of **receive:** *They received a notice about what to recycle and where to put it.*

### remarkable

Deserving notice, or outstanding: *The landing on the moon was a **remarkable** event.*

### remove

To take out, take away: *You can **remove** the seeds of the apple after you slice it.*

### repeat

To do or say again: *Please **repeat** the directions and I will try to follow them.*

### repeated

A form of **repeat:** *The game was so much fun that they **repeated** it the next day.*

### result

Something that happens because of something else: *The class mural was a **result** of days of planning and painting.*

### roar

To make a loud, deep sound or noise: *Engines **roar** and wheels roll before the planes take off.*

### roared

A form of **roar:** *When the lion **roared**, the smaller animals turned and ran.*

### root

The part of a plant that grows down into the ground: *You cannot see the **root** of a plant because it is underground.*

# S

## search

To look over or go through carefully: *We will **search** along the path for the missing gloves.*

## sense

Clear reason or good judgment: *It makes **sense** to wear boots in deep snow.*

## sensible

A form of **sense:** *Be **sensible** enough to take an extra swimsuit on vacation.*

## serious

Thoughtful, important, not joking: *This is a **serious** topic, so please listen carefully.*

## seriously

A form of **serious:** *If you take it **seriously**, you should practice the piano every day.*

## serve

To prepare and offer something: *We used trays to help us carry and **serve** the tea at the party.*

serve

## served

A form of **serve:** *The waitress **served** the desserts last.*

## sharp

Having a fine point or cutting edge: *The knives are **sharp**, so please be careful.*

## sharpening

A form of **sharp:** *By **sharpening** the pencil, he could draw very fine lines.*

### shoot

A plant that has just begun to grow up through the soil: *I was happy to see the **shoot** of my plant poke through the dirt.*

### slippery

Slick or likely to cause slipping: *The rain froze overnight so the streets were **slippery**.*

### soak

To make something completely wet by placing it in liquid or by pouring liquid on it: *The heavy rain will **soak** the soil.*

### soften

To make something softer or less hard: *The ice cream began to **soften** because I left it on the counter.*

### sore

Painful or feeling hurt: *The shoes were so tight that she had a **sore** toe.*

### souvenir

Something kept to recall a special time or place: *I wish that I had a **souvenir** from the trip.*

**souvenir**

### spin

To twist cotton or wool to make yarn or thread: *We learned to **spin** thread when we studied how families lived long ago.*

### spinning

A form of **spin**: *While **spinning** the yarn, she hummed a tune.*

**sprang**

A form of **spring:** *The fox sprang out of the tall grass and chased the chipmunk.*

**spring**

To leap, or move up in a quick motion: *The squirrels spring from the tree to the porch roof.*

**stare**

To look with a steady, often wide-eyed gaze: *Many people don't like to have someone stare at them.*

**staring**

A form of **stare:** *Everybody was staring at the huge box and guessing what was inside.*

**startle**

To cause a sudden movement, as of surprise: *Talking might startle the deer, so be very quiet.*

**startled**

A form of **startle:** *The ducks were startled by the truck and flew away.*

**steer**

To guide or direct the course of: *I'm glad that we learned to steer the boat.*

**strand**

One of the long pieces that are twisted together to make rope or yarn: *The strong rope was made from many strands.*

**stream**

A body of water that flows in a bed or channel: *A few miles from here, that small trickle of water turns into a flowing stream.*

**studied**

A form of **study:** *Long ago sailors studied the stars by watching the sky at night.*

**study**

To try to learn from, or to look closely at: *They study the ant farm to find out how ants work together.*

**suspicious**

Not trusting, or having doubts: *We were* **suspicious** *because last time she tried to fool us.*

**suspiciously**

A form of **suspicious:** *The mouse watched the snake* **suspiciously** *from far off.*

**swift**

Fast: *A* **swift** *rabbit can run away from a hungry fox.*

# T

**tangle**

Snarl or twist: *We* **tangle** *the string every time we try to fly our kite.*

**tangled**

A form of **tangle:** *The kittens played with the* **tangled** *ball of yarn.*

**task**

A job or chore: *Cleaning my messy room is a difficult* **task**!

**tasty**

Having a lot of good flavor: *I asked for more of my grandmother's* **tasty** *soup.*

**taught**

A form of **teach:** *My grandma* **taught** *me how to build a birdhouse.*

**teach**

To give knowledge or lessons: *I can* **teach** *you how to do that kind of puzzle.*

**tear**

To pull apart or rip: *I like to* **tear** *colored paper and make designs.*

**tearing**

A form of **tear:** *After* **tearing** *down the old barn, they built a newer, stronger one.*

## toss

To throw or pitch: *In this game, you **toss** balls into a basket.*

**toss**

## tossed

A form of **toss:** *The two children **tossed** the beanbag back and forth.*

## train

To teach skills or ways to act: *You can **train** your dog to wait quietly.*

## training

A form of **train:** *After many weeks of **training**, the team won every game.*

## trouble

Something that is difficult, dangerous, or upsetting: *He didn't want to cause **trouble**, so he worked very carefully.*

## tumble

To roll or do somersaults: *Mikael likes to **tumble** all the way down that steep hill!*

## tumbling

A form of **tumble:** *After **tumbling** across the mat, the gymnast did a split and a cartwheel.*

# U

## upset

To be disturbed or turned over: *The birds were **upset** when the cat climbed toward their nest.*

# V

## valuable

Important, or worth a lot of money: *Be careful to not break the antique plate. It is very **valuable**.*

### village

A group of houses that make up a community smaller than a town: *There were about fifty people in the whole village.*

# W

### waterproof

Able to keep water off or out: *For hiking in the rain, you need a raincoat and a waterproof hat.*

### weave

To pass something such as yarn or twigs over and under one another: *The children learned how to weave a small basket.*

### web

Material that connects or ties together: *The spider spun a web between two branches of the tree.*

### webbed

A form of **web:** *Ducks, geese, and penguins have webbed feet.*

**webbed**

### whistle

Something that makes a high, clear sound when air is blown through it: *The coach blew a whistle when he wanted the team to stop and listen.*

### wisdom

Being able to judge what is best and right: *People say that you gain wisdom after many years of living and making mistakes.*

**wonder**

To be curious about: *I wonder how birds feel when they are flying.*

**worn**

Damaged by being used too much: *My little brother's blanket looks very **worn** because he takes it with him wherever he goes.*

# Y

**yarn**

Spun wool or nylon for weaving or knitting: *She loved the colors and feel of the **yarn** in the knitting store.*

**yarn**

# Acknowledgments

## Main Literature Selections

*Dex: The Heart of a Hero* by Caralyn Buehner, illustrated by Mark Buehner. Text copyright ©2004 by Caralyn Buehner. Illustrations copyright ©2004 by Mark Buehner. All rights reserved. Reprinted by permission of HarperCollins Publishers.

*The Dog that Dug for Dinosaurs* by Shirley Raye Redmond, illustrated by Simon Sullivan. Text copyright ©2004 by Shirley Raye Redmond. Illustrations copyright ©2004 by Simon Sullivan. Reprinted by permission of Aladdin Paperbacks, an imprint of Simon & Schuster's Children's Publishing Division. All rights reserved.

Excerpt from *Exploring Space Travel* by Laura Hamilton Waxman. Copyright ©2012 by Lerner Publishing Group, Inc. Reprinted by permission of Lerner Publishing Group, Inc.

*From Seed to Plant* by Gail Gibbons. Copyright ©1991 by Gall Gibbons. All rights reserved. Reprinted by permission of Holiday House, Inc.

"Gloria Who Might Be My Best Friend" from *The Stories Julian Tells* by Ann Cameron. Text copyright ©1981 by Ann Cameron. All rights reserved. Reprinted by permission of Random House Children's Books, a division of Random House, Inc., and Ann Cameron.

*The Goat in the Rug* by Charles L. Blood and Martin Link, illustrated by Nancy Winslow Parker. Text copyright ©1976 by Charles L. Blood and Martin A. Link. Illustrations copyright ©1976 by Nancy Winslow Parker. Reprinted by permission of Simon & Schuster Books for Young Readers, an Imprint of Simon & Schuster Children's Publishing Division. All rights reserved.

*Half-Chicken/Mediopollito* by Ala Flor Ada, illustrated by Kim Howard. Text copyright ©1995 by Ala Flor Ada. Illustrations copyright ©1995 by Kim Howard. Reprinted by permission of BookStop Literary Agency, LLC.

"Keep a Poem in Your Pocket" from *Something Special* by Beatrice Schenk de Reginers. Text copyright ©1958, 1986 by Beatrice Schenk de Reginers. Reprinted by permission of Marian Reiner, Literary Agent.

*Luke Goes to Bat* by Rachel Isadora. Copyright ©2005 by Rachel Isadora. Reprinted by permission of G. P. Putnam's Sons, a division of Penguin Young Readers Group, a member of Penguin Group (USA) Inc. All rights reserved.

*Mr. Tanen's Tie Trouble* written and illustrated by Maryann Cocca-Lefler. Text and illustrations copyright ©2003 by Maryann Cocca-Lefler. Adapted by permission of Albert Whitman & Company.

*My Name is Gabriela/Me Ilamo Gabriela* by Monica Brown, illustrated by John Parra. Text copyright ©2005 by Monica Brown. Illustrations copyright ©by John Para, Vicki Prentice Associates, Inc. NYC. Translations ©2005 by Luna Rising, a division of Cooper Square Publishing. Reprinted by permission of Rowman & Littlefield Publishing Group.

*The Mysterious Tadpole* written and illustrated by Steven Kellogg. Copyright ©2002 by Steven Kellogg. All rights reserved including the right of reproduction in whole or in part in any form. Reprinted by permission of Dial Books for Young Readers, a member of Penguin's Young Readers Group, a division of Penguin Group (USA) Inc.

*Now & Ben: The Modern Inventions of Benjamin Franklin* by Gene Barretta. Copyright ©2006 by Gene Barretta. All rights reserved. Reprinted by permission of Henry Holt and Company LLC.

*Penguin Chick* by Betty Tatham, illustrated by Helen K. Davie. Text copyright ©2002 by Betty Tatham. Illustrations copyright ©2002 by Helen K. Davie. All rights reserved. Reprinted by permission of HarperCollins Children's Books, a division of HarperCollins Publishers.

"The Period" from *On Your Marks: A Package of Punctuation* by Richard Armour. Text copyright ©1969 by Richard Armour. Reprinted by permission of Geoffrey Armour, who controls all rights.

"Share the Adventure" by Patricia and Frederick McKissack. Text copyright ©1993 by Patricia and Frederick McKissak. First appeared as a National Children's Book Week Poem by The Children's Book Council. Reprinted by permission of Curtis Brown, Ltd.

*The Signmaker's Assistant* written and illustrated by Tedd Arnold. Copyright ©1992 by Tedd Arnold. All rights reserved. Reprinted by permission of Dial Books for Young Readers, a member of

# Credits

## Photo Credits

**Placement Key:** (r) right, (l) left, (c) center, (t) top, (b) bottom, (bg) background

**2** (tl) ©Leland Bobbe/Getty Images; **2** (cl) ©Bettmann/Corbis; **3** (cl) Corbis; **3** (tl) AP Images; **4** (tl) Getty Images; **4** (cl) Sean Justice/Getty; **5** (tl) ©Ethnologisches Museum, Staatliche Museen, Berlin, Germany/Dietrich Graf/Art Resource; **5** (bl) Andreas Stirnberg; **6** (tl) Michael Gadomski/Animals Animals-Earth Scenes; **6** (cl) Mark Polott/Jupiter Images; **7** (cl) © Stock Montage/Contributor/Hulton Archive/Getty Images **8** ©Julien Tromeur/Shutterstock; **9** ©©Stokkete/Shutterstock; **10** (c) Masterfile; **10** (b) © Jim Cummins/Taxi/Getty Images; **10** ©Leland Bobbe/Getty Images; **11** (tr) Tim Hall/Getty; **11** (cl) Rolf Bruderer/Corbis; **11** (cr) © Blend Images/Alamy; **11** (bl) Robert W. Ginn / Alamy; **11** (br) Ronnie Kaufman/Age Fotostock; **12** ©Getty Images; **40** (b) ©Dorling Kindersley/Getty Images; **40** (tl) ©Leland Bobbe/Getty Images; **41** ©Leland Bobbe/Getty Images; **41** (t) ©Richard Hutchings/Photo Researchers, Inc.; **42** (t) ©Photodisc/Getty Images; **43** (t) ©Brand X Pictures/Getty Images; **43** (tl) ©Leland Bobbe/Getty Images; **47** (br) Rubberball/Jupiter Images/Getty; **48** (c) Ron Chapple; **48** (b) Masterfile; **48** (tc) ©Bettmann/CORBIS; **48** David Madison/Corbis; **49** (tl) Ted Grant/Masterfile; **49** (tr) Tom & Dee Ann McCarthy/Corbis; **49** (cl) Yellow Dog Productions/Getty; **49** (cr) Holly Harris/Getty; **49** (bl) Tom & Dee Ann McCarthy/Corbis; **49** (br) Photos.com/Alamy; **50** ©Photodisc/Getty Images; **77** (c) ©Yellow Dog Productions/Getty Images; **78** (b) Getty Images; **78** (bg) David Madison/Corbis; **78** (bg) ©Lake County Museum/Corbis; **78** (tl) ©Bettmann/CORBIS; **78** (border) David Madison/Corbis; **79** (b) Bettmann/Corbis; **80** (bg) ©Paul Buck/EPA/Corbis; **80** (br) ©Bettmann/Corbis; **80** (bg) David Madison/Corbis; **81** (b) Getty Images/Photodisc; **81** (cr) ©Bettmann/Corbis; **81** (tc) ©Bettmann/Corbis; **81** (tc) David Madison/Corbis; **85** (br) Masterfile; **86** (c) ©David Buffington/Getty Images; **86** (b) Masterfile; **87** (tl) Corbis; **87** (tr) JUPITERIMAGES/ Thinkstock/Alamy; **87** (cr) SW Productions/Brand X/Corbis; **87** (bl) moodboard/Corbis; **87** (br) Bob Sciarrino/Corbis; **87** (cl) ©Doctor Stock/Getty Images; **89** ©Comstock Images/Getty Images; **111** (t) ©Don Farrall/Getty Images; **117** (c) ©Blend Images/Alamy Images; **121** (br) Digital Vision/Alamy; **122** (c) Jonathan Blair/Corbis; **122** (b) Mitch York/Getty; **123** (tl) Zak Waters / Alamy; **123** (tr) Masterfile; **123** (cr) Jan Tadeusz / Alamy; **123** (bl) ©Blend Images/Alamy Images; **123** (br) Benjamin Rondel/Getty; **124** ©Visions of America, LLC/Alamy Images; **151** ©Jupiter Images/Brand X/Alamy Images; **157** (t) ©Phil Degginger/Alamy Images; **161** (br) Masterfile; **162** (c) Digital Vision Ltd./SuperStock; **162** (b) Juniors Bildarchiv / Alamy; **162** (tc) AP Images; **162** (tc) CORBIS; **163** (tl) Juniors Bildarchiv / Alamy; **163** (tr) David Schmidt/Masterfile; **163** (cl) DLILLC/Corbis; **163** (cr) Don Smetzer/Getty; **163** (bl) Myrleen Ferguson Cate / PhotoEdit; **163** (br) Thomas Schweizer/Masterfile; **165** ©MBI/Alamy Images; **191** ©Abrams/Lacagnina/Getty Images; **194** (bg) AP Images; **194** (tl) AP Images; **194** (tl) CORBIS; **195** (br) NASA; **195** (r) NASA/JPL-Caltech/GSFC/SDSS; **195** (c) CORBIS; **196** (br) ©Wendy Connett/Getty Images; **196** (bg) ©Photodisc/Getty Images; **197** (cr) Getty; **197** (tc) AP Images; **197** (tc) CORBIS; **201** (br) Masterfile; **204** ©Blend Images/Ariel Skelley/Vetta/Getty Images; **205** ©Rita Kochmarjova/Shutterstock; **206** (cr) ©Tim Mason/Alamy Images; **206** (b) Enrique R. Aguirre Aves / Alamy; **206** (tc) Getty Images; **207** (tl) Peter Beavis/Getty; **207** (tr) Kim Westerskov/Getty; **207** (cl) Terry Andrewartha/naturepl.com; **207** (cr) © Corbis Premium RF/Alamy; **207** (bl) © Graphic Science / Alamy; **207** (br) Arco Images GmbH / Alamy; **208** moodboard/Alamy; **212** (c) ©Peter